Oak Tree Tales

Published by Bob Bancks
Blue Grass, Iowa
www.iowafarmboy.net
bob.bancks@gmail.com

Bob Bancks
Blue Grass, Iowa
www.iowafarmboy.net
bob.bancks@gmail.com

Edits by Misty Urban
Sketches Created by Patricia Mortiz
Graphic Design by Emily Heim, Expressions by Em

Printed in the United States of America
First Publication: October 2017
ISBN # 978-1975977993

Table of Contents

Before It Rains

"Gee, it is such a beautiful day. I can't believe it supposed to rain late this afternoon. I guess I'll find out. I'm not going anywhere soon. I don't know how I was so stupid. Driving so close to the edge of the creek just to see how much water was in it and Zowie! The creek bank gave away. I tried to jump clear, but got caught in the steering wheel. Now here I am, one leg under the rear wheel of the tractor. If it is going to rain I hope Sherry gets here before it does.

I'm sure glad we got the hay made yesterday. It has been a struggle getting it made this summer. The weather just hasn't been dry enough for hay making. Barely had three days in a row of warm sunshine. I think tomorrow I'll clean some lots. The south slope on the alfalfa field was sure weak. Maybe a little manure will help. Of course, it will depend on how wet the field is. Speaking of rain, look at those clouds in the southwest. They are building up. I sure hope Sherry realizes I'm not in the barn. I should have told her I was going to the pasture. I hope she gets here before it rains.

I've heard of old guys upsetting tractors and getting hurt or killed. I never thought it would happen to me. I should have gotten off and looked instead of being so lazy. Now here I am stuck under this wheel.

My leg is probably broken, but I don't feel much pain. Sherry will have to go back to the house and get Dad or a neighbor to free me. First, she has to get here before it rains.

I guess I'll have to be patient. It's only four o'clock. Sherry will miss me soon. Let me see, the oats will start heading out soon. I checked the seeding yesterday and it looks terrific. Maybe I should use the oats for silage instead of grain and straw. Those clouds are sure building up and the air is really humid. The next worry is hail or high winds. It can surely cause a lot of damage. I hate it when the oats gets flattened by heavy rain and strong wind. This creek is small now, but it does rise quickly. I've seen where it's been four or five feet deep. I sure hope Sherry gets here before it rains.

The cows should be coming home for milking soon. I'm sure Sherry will miss me then. She'll start looking for me. Did I hear thunder? I can't see much over the hill. I don't know if I can raise up enough to stay above the water level. I don't mind getting wet, but I certainly don't want to drown. I sure hope Sherry gets here before it rains"

This short essay was my first attempt at writing. It was written for an English class at my community college. In those days, they were called junior colleges. I wrote the story to the best of my memory because copying machines and scanning devices were not available in 1959. The professor, Dr. Keith Larson, read my story before the class. He asked if he could keep my paper and I said, "Sure." Not realizing that someday I might want to read it again. I'm told he read it to several classes in later years. Oh yes, I received an 'A' grade on the piece.

For those who might be interested. Muscatine Junior College was located in the old Franklin Grade school building on Grandview Avenue. The president was James Loper. My math professor was Louise Gackle, chemistry 101 was Gerald Koch, Biology 101 was Ted Allen, and Language Skills was Dr. Keith Larson. At that time, many students attended Muscatine Junior College for one year only since most second year courses were not recognized by the major universities.

The School House Well

One room country schools were built before the days of modern plumbing. If fact, most farm houses lacked running water except for maybe a pump connected to a rain water cistern, so it stands to reason the country schools would be the same. My school, Hazel Dell #3 was located in eastern Muscatine County. It was one of four schools in my township. Three were basically the same, the one in the village of Montpelier had two rooms and plumbing, at least, when I was attending Hazel Dell. There is nothing left at the school site except the well. The property was sold and a house was moved in. The owners decided to keep the old pump and platform for a conversational piece.

The well was hand dug many years ago. It was lined with bricks down its entire depth. The depth, I've told at about 50 or 60 feet. A hand pump was installed to draw up the water. With each stroke of the handle, a series of leather washers would pull the water up through a pipe, but would restrict it from returning down to the bottom. If you pumped long and fast enough, water would eventually reach the top and flow out the spigot. The faster you pumped the more came out, in the case for school, the bigger the kid the faster the flow.

When I first attended Hazel Dell, the well was covered with a wooden platform made of planks. Any water spilled would simply run back down into the well through the cracks between the planks. This did not cause any alarm for anyone attending school because this was how it was at home. Even when we washed our muddy boots the silt laden water would filter through the cracks and to the bottom of the well. Many times frogs or toads would crawl through the cracks at the edge and disappear into the depths only to be pumped to the surface later. When such an event took place, the pumper would just pump a little longer to make sure the water was 'pure' again.

The first day of school generally was also the first day the well had been used since Spring. Many times field mice had taken up residence in the housing of the pump. To the mouse's surprise the surge of water would flush him or her out of the otherwise safe environment. It would scurry out all wet and bug-eyed. We would try and step on the dazed critter, but generally it would escape. I can only remember one garter snake slithering out of the spigot. These episodes were only experienced the first day of school since after then the well was used often enough to keep out unwanted guests.

The one room schools were ruled by the local school board, which was your dad, my dad and someone else's dad. It wasn't until the county superintendent's office or the state office of education started to demand a better regulation of the water supply, did our water supply change. First, improvement was a concrete cap or lid over the well. No longer could the water return to the well through the cracks. Frogs and toads did not stumble into the precipice become part of the contents. Field mice still made their homes in the pump during the summer and had to be evicted each Fall.

The real demise of the well came when a family from Davenport moved into our community. Their dad had the audacity to have the water checked for purity. Of course, it was contaminated. Yet I don't believe anyone had ever gotten sick because of the water. To correct the well problem, the authorities dumped chlorine tablets into the well. They fixed it all right. The water tasted yucky for several weeks. The older boys, not girls, would pump the water just enough so it was drinkable. I mean some days after a long weekend they'd pump for twenty or thirty minutes. The treatment lasted for many months then was forgotten about and the water returned to its original state.

Now I suppose you are wondering how we got the drinking water into the school building. This was a daily chore for the older students. We had a large crock with a button spigot at the bottom. You would hold your glass or cup under it. Push the button and get your drink. This water crock had be re-filled every day. Some days when the weather was bad, the teacher would allow for a carry-over day. Everyone had his or hers private cup, but they all set on the same shelf from one drink to the next. Once in a great while we would take our cup home to have it washed. One year someone, probably from the superintendent's office, had the great idea to use paper cups. You know those little cone shaped ones which look like an ice cream cone. This was to protect the student's health and well being. The idea worked fine until someone decided we were using too many cups. To remedy the situation, we were each issued one cup per week. Guess what? The cups were placed on the same shelf as the old cups only they all looked the same. We tried writing our name on the cups, but that was unsuccessful. Mix-ups were common. Another problem was the cups after four or five use, they began to leak out the pointy bottom. Needless to say the sanitary cup idea didn't last long, so much for modern ideas.

By today's standards, our water was unfit to drink. All those kids before me survived and so did I. It seems the shiny cool water fountains of today are taken for granted in our schools. We thought our water was as pure and cold when it came from the depths of our old well. The pump still stands on the concrete platform poured so many years ago. I stopped and tried it last summer. As always, I roused a resident field mouse, but soon the cool water began to flow out the old spigot. Memories of the pump and Hazel Dell #3 flowed that day. Some things never change.

A Brotherhood of Farmers

There is a fraternity in this country which does not have a Greek letter in its name. Neither does it have animals as its symbol. At one time it was the largest employer in the nation, but now less than 2 percent of the population call it their occupation. One may not identify it as a fraternity because it contains such a varied population and is spread from Maine to California. This fraternity is the American farming community, and it includes all the farmers who make their living entirely from the land. Until recent years this fraternity was solely a male organization, but lately a few women have cracked the gender barrier.

Six years ago, I met a fellow farmer who became a close friend. The unusual part of the relationship is that we were 1,100 miles apart.

I met Cliff on his dairy farm just outside the little town of Danville in northeast Vermont. I was in Vermont as a guest of a friend who graciously offered her wonderful summer home to my cousins for a family reunion. The group was out on an excursion one morning to a pie shop located on his farm. This pie shop is unusual, for it is just a small building alongside a country road. It is a serve-yourself pie shop. The pies plus doughnuts and coffee are always available. Just stop in and have a bite. The cash register is a cigar box. You make your own change. If you are a neighboring farmer on a tractor, you just add it to your tab. This is the way Vermonters do business in rural areas. It was behind this small chicken coop-sized building where I met Cliff Langmade.

Cliff was not a large person, maybe 5 foot, 9 inches tall with a slight frame. He had dark wavy hair with a touch of gray. It was his smile which made him so special and, of course, the New England brogue. We greeted each other and soon discovered we had something in common. We both belonged to this great fraternity of farmers. I caught his attention when I asked if the manure pit behind his dairy barn was large enough to hold a year's production. The conversation changed to the wrapped hay bales on the side of the lot. From there, we discussed, corn, hogs, and dairy cows. Soybeans, which they grow very little of in Vermont, were the crop he was most interested in. The soybean meal he used for his dairy animals had to be trucked from Ohio. This made the product very expensive. As my cousins waited in the shade eating homemade doughnuts and drinking Green Mountain coffee, we continued our conversation. He was as interested in my operation as I was in his.

I visited Cliff's dairy farm three times since that meeting, each time forging our growing friendship. Even though 1,100 miles separated us, we kept in contact. He called me every few months and we compared notes. He'd ask about the size of my corn planter and other equipment. He had seen pictures of these huge planters and combines which farmers in the Midwest use. He claimed if he had one of those big planters, it would be two times around the field and he'd be done. He had to plant 80-day corn and it might still get frosted in mid-September. He couldn't raise alfalfa because of the very cold winters. Orchard grass and clovers were the forage of choice. Two hundred plus bushels of corn to the acre was unheard of. He always had to purchase extra corn for feeding. All his corn acres went for silage. I invited Cliff to visit Iowa, but I knew he would never leave his little piece of Heaven in Vermont.

I promised Cliff I would return shortly after my last visit, but time has a way of slipping away and soon one year turned into two. I yearned to go back, but my sister needed me in California because she had a hip replaced. It would be another year.

Last September, I received an email from Cliff's sister. Cliff had been diagnosed with ALS. This was a shock to me for he seemed so healthy. He entered Massachusetts General Hospital in Boston, a major research hospital dealing with ALS. Cliff knew what was ahead, for one of his sisters and a nephew had already succumbed to this dreaded disease. When he called in early October, he told me he probably would not see Christmas since his right arm was already numb. I was surprised when he called in early January. He had been accepted to try a new drug program to combat the disease. He was one of 30 patients in the world to receive this treatment. He was excited. In March he called again. He believed he could feel a tingling in his affected right arm. Maybe the drugs were working.

On Mother's Day weekend, we talked once more. He just had to tell me he had received the Distinguished Holstein Breeders Award. He now had survived 10 months since his diagnosis, longer than most patients. His right arm was still numb, but he could still drive a tractor and his pickup. If this was the worst, he could live with it. He claimed he was taking so many different pills, he had to chart each one as to when and how many. But his life looked promising.

In June, I received an email from my friend who had provided the house we lived in. She had spoken with Cliff's sister, Sue. Cliff was not doing well. The promise of the miracle drug was fading. Cliff's left arm was becoming numb, next would be his chest and neck. Finally, he would not be able to speak or eat. He would be kept alive for a while with intravenous feeding, but as the disease progressed, his lungs would be affected and he would suffocate. The saddest consquence of this disease is that his mind would remain sharp. He knew his health was deteriorating, but he could do nothing to stop it.

Jane and I visited Cliff in late July. He could talk and walk. His arms hung limply at his sides. When we were leaving, he asked us to hug him. This was difficult, since he couldn't hug back. That evening we attended a community potluck held in our honor. We said our good-byes for the last time. There many tears from all of us.

After we returned to Iowa two weeks later, we received a call from Cliff's sister. Cliff had been re-admitted to Massachusetts General. He did return home for his last days. Two weeks later, as my wife and I were relaxing in our porch swing, we received the call we dreaded. Cliff had passed away.

I am glad to be a part of this wonderful fraternity to which I belong. Because of it, I've been able to be part of the life of this dairyman from Vermont. He and I had a common bond of dirty hands, sweaty brows, and love of the land God had created for us.

Thank you, Cliff, for the wonderful conversations these past years, May God bless you and all your wonderful Vermont friends.

July Visitor

Author's note: This is a true story. It came to me as a vision or dream. My dad was as real as real could be.

It was a warm late July evening. Jane, my wife, and I had just put in a long day of freezing sweet corn. We sat in the living room in our pajamas, waiting for the evening news. Jane decided she was too tired to wait.

"Tell me about it tomorrow morning. I'm going to bed," she told me, and left for the bedroom at the opposite end of the house.

I turned the TV volume down and continued to watch. While sitting in my favorite chair, I heard a strange knock. I called softly, "Jane, is that you?"

There was no reply. I got up and walked down the hall to check. I looked in on her and she was sound asleep. I quietly closed the bedroom door and returned to the living room, I heard the knock again. It came from the front door. I peered through the oval frosted glass of the door and saw the shadow of a man standing outside.

Who could it be at this hour? I thought. *Maybe someone needs help.*

I turned on the porch light. Yes, there was someone out there. I opened the door slowly.

"May I help you?"

"Bob."

"Yes."

I opened the door wider and looked at the man in the dim light. He looked familiar. He stood there in his brown suede jacket and green wool tie. I racked my brain for the place I had seen this person. I studied his face and stammered, "D—d--dad?"

"Yes. Do you remember me?"

"Yes, but it has been over sixty years. Would you like to come in?"

He entered the living room and scanned the surroundings. He looked at the watch hanging in the display case on the mantel.

"That's your watch, Dad."

"I know," he replied.

"The folding ruler was from Shorty Mueller, one of the carpenters who built the house. The picture is you and Mom on your wedding day."

He turned to me and smiled again. "I know, Bob."

He continued to review the mantel, the library, and the mementos in the hutch. The furniture had changed and the walls were a different color.

My mind flowed back to his last days here at the farm. That terrible Sunday morning, he was on the ladder cleaning out the rain gutter on the barn. The ladder slipped on the damp concrete. He fell twenty feet to the ground. He should have been in the house getting ready for church and relaxing, but he thought he had time to do a little job.

In the house, Mom started to worry. Dad was going to be late again. My sister and I were listening to our favorite Sunday morning radio program, "White Rabbit Bus." We had the radio on a little loud and were singing at the top of our lungs. Mom finally went outside and called, "Carl! Carl! You're going to be late."

She heard a call from the barn. "Help! Help!" She dashed to the barn and found Dad lying in the feed room. He had pulled himself inside because all his hollering did not attract his family, but it sure did attract the sows. They thought he was going to feed them. How he lifted his broken body two feet straight up was a miracle. He knew he had broken his hip and maybe more.

"Get me to the house," he told her.

"But how, Carl?" she asked.

"Have Bobby drive the Ford tractor down here and maybe I can sit on the drawbar."

Mom ran back to the house and got me and my sister. She told me to get the Ford tractor and come to the dairy barn. Dad had fallen.

I was ten years old at the time. Women were not supposed to drive tractors in the fifties. The three of us helped to lift Dad onto the tractor drawbar and slowly we inched our way to the front door. Mom and my sister, Mary, helped to carry his leg. Dad had to be in a lot of pain. We didn't call the ambulance, because they were almost non-existent in rural Iowa in the 1950s. Funeral hearses doubled as ambulances many times. We lifted and worked Dad to the couch in the living room. She insisted that Dad have on clean clothes before she took him to the hospital. She and Mary struggled to get him into clean overalls and shirt. She called our neighbor, Wayne Kraft, to help load Dad into the backseat of the Studebaker. She and Dad headed for the hospital in Davenport.

Mary and I went to church with our neighbors. After church, our grandparents took us to their house for lunch. We waited with my aunts, uncles, and cousins for Mom to return. She drove into Grandpa's farmyard at five o'clock.

"Dad has a broken hip. Because of the swelling, they will not be able to operate and set the bone until later in the week," she explained as if there was nothing to worry about. At least he wasn't going to die. By mid-week it was determined Friday would be the day for the surgery.

Friday was warm for late October. At my one-room school, I was playing baseball with the other fifteen kids when my uncle's car stopped outside the school house. He went inside to talk to Miss Kemper. She came out to get me and told me to go with my uncle. I was surprised, but followed orders. Inside his big Oldsmobile was my sister; he had picked her up from high school.

Mary and I were quiet. We didn't ask questions. We raced to Davenport and the hospital. Inside the hospital, we hurried through the halls. This was unusual, because children under fourteen were not allowed beyond the entryway in the 50s. I was excited when we reached Dad's room. I was going to see my dad. Instead, there was an empty bed. Mom stood beside it, crying.

"Your father is dead," she said. Mary and I couldn't believe what she was telling us. It wasn't possible. Dad was always there when we needed him. Now what?

The weather changed by the time we reached home. A cold front moved through Iowa, and a strong wind blew in from the northwest. Because it was the weekend, I wanted to go back to the schoolhouse and retrieve my bicycle. It was a tough ride home. I remember passing my school friends, who asked why I left school early. I told them they would find out when they got home. I was too upset to tell them the real answer.

Sunday visitations were not held in the 50s. The visitation began Monday and lasted for two days. Dad was fifty-one years old and well known in both Muscatine and Scott Counties. Hundreds of people attended. When we returned Tuesday evening from the second day of visitation, I asked my mother, Daddy isn't coming home again, is he?"

She confirmed my question, and I went into hysterics. It took my grandfather and my mother two hours to calm me down. Grandfather stayed over and slept with me that night.

It was cold and windy the day of the funeral. There were so many attendees at the service, some stood outside. It was bitterly cold at the graveside. Then it was over.

That was 1951. This is now. Dad was here, right my living room. Well, really, it was his living room. Was I dreaming?

"Do you have time to sit and talk, Dad?" I asked.

"Some," he answered. "How are things going? You know I never met your wife."

"You would have loved Jane, Dad. She was a city girl, but she became a great farmwife. She can drive tractors and equipment as good as any man. She loves this farm. She's asleep right now. Do you want me to wake her?"

"No. How about your children?"

"Three boys. none are going to continue to farm. I'm going to be the last Bancks to actively farm. The two youngest, Jon and Eric, never really wanted to farm. Blaine tried when he came out of college. Prices and economic downturn made it difficult to keep him here. I also worked him too hard and was not able to pay him enough. After four years, he left for another job. He became a sales rep for a coop in central Iowa. He has done very well. I'm sorry, Dad, but I couldn't do any better at that the time."

"Son," he replied, "don't fret over it. Every farm has a beginning and an ending. Some are just a little faster than others. You have taken good care of the land. In the whole scheme of things, it is not important. The Bancks' have had a good run."

"Thanks, Dad. That is a great weight off my shoulders. I hated it when Blaine left. I couldn't blame him, though. With the debt we had, I just couldn't pay him enough."

We talked for about another hour. He asked about Mary and her family. He asked about my two uncles. When he married Mom, he became closer to my uncles than his own family. He traded work and machinery with my uncle Jim. Finally he announced, "I better be going. I'm only allowed a short time here."

As he rose from his chair, I asked, "Do you get to see Mom up in heaven?"

"Oh yes, once in a while, but you see, Bob, it's different there. It's kind of difficult to explain. We are all just spirits. We aren't married anymore. We are just one big family living with God. She does get in touch with me now and then. She is happy and doesn't worry anymore. The next time I see her, I'll tell her you asked. Now, I must be going."

He started for the front door. I followed. We stood on the porch a minute. I shook his hand with his bum finger. A burst of breeze blew the door open behind us. I turned to shut it. When I turned back, he was gone. A breeze flowed across the corn field, rippling the leaves of the stalks. It was like he was checking the field for the last time.

"Have a nice trip back, Dad. Thanks for coming," I called, my voice cracking.

Now many may not believe what I have just told you. But it is true and vivid to me. Was it a vision or a dream? I don't know. But I believe my Dad returned to see me and forgive me. You can believe what you want.

South Dakota Snow Bound

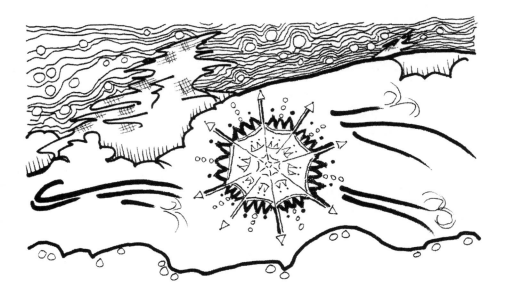

Author's Note: This is a true story as told to me by my mother. My father and Fred Thoene (pronounced "Tay-ney") were first cousins and great friends. Even though they lived 400 miles apart, they traveled together and had a very close bond. My mother and Lillie, Fred's wife, also became close friends. All the persons involved have passed away and no real record of what took place is available, so I took the writer's prerogative and embellished the story, reflecting what might have happened at that time in South Dakota.

It was a cold, clear day in Bonesteel, South Dakota, a small rural town in the center of the state, about thirty miles west of the Missouri River. About 500 people lived there, plus several dogs and cats. Main Street was paved, but the side streets were gravel at best, and some were mud. It was 1925 and just two weeks before Valentine's Day.

Lillie Thoene had driven nine miles into town to get groceries and other supplies. In the window of the grocery store she saw an advertisement for a Valentine Gala Dance to be held Odd Fellows Hall. The band playing that evening was her favorite, Sid Carpenter and the Sawbucks. She read the sign twice to be sure she remembered the date and time. She hurried through the store and dashed over to the ladies' dress shop across the street. Lillie hadn't cleared it with her husband Fred yet, but she was sure he would say yes.

It didn't take her long to realize the frock she was looking for would not be found in Bonesteel. She'd have to convince Fred to take her to Gregory or Winner for a new dress. She re-crossed the wide street and opened the door to her 1925 Dodge Custom sedan. It was a fancy auto with white walls, velour seats, and an electric starter. Just before she slammed the door, Julie Lund, Lillie's cousin, hollered from the upstairs window above the dress shop.

"Hey, Lillie, are you and Fred coming to the Valentine Gala?"

"Most certainly. I haven't told Fred yet but he will know as soon as I get home."

"I saw you at my shop. Did you see anything you liked?"

Lillie hated to disappoint her cousin, so she lied. "Yeah, there was a couple, but I have to ask Fred first."

"Well, come back on Tuesday. I have a whole new shipment coming in. I went to Sioux Falls and picked out of the latest fashions from Chicago. You ought to see them! They are short, sleek and sexy. And they have matching hats."

"Okay, I'll see you Tuesday."

Lillie hurried out Highway 18 and turned onto the road to the Thoene ranch, located five miles to the south. She stopped at the row of mailboxes. A big box sitting on the ground was addressed to Rosy Two Hats. Rosy and her husband, Hiram, were Native Americans who lived just north of the Thoenes. When the federal government downsized the Rosebud Indian Reservation, all Native Americans were allowed to keep 40 acres for their own. Most rented their ground to surrounding ranchers and lived on about three acres.

Hiram was different. He chose to raise colored sheep. His wife sheared the sheep and spun the fiber into wool yarn, then wove the yarn into blankets and throws. At first, Rosy did everything, but now she sent the wool to a processer and they cleaned and spun the wool into skeins for her use. Lillie figured the box contained more yarn. As was the custom with her neighbors, they all delivered each other's mail. She loaded the box into the car. She would drop it off as she passed Hiram's house.

The mud road was rutted from the winter thaws and freezing. Lillie held the steering wheel tightly. It was all she could do to keep the car from being thrown into the ditch by the deep ruts. In the spring, these same ruts would be a quagmire of mud until the frost left the ground and Fred could drag the road to smooth it. It was a county road, but ranchers took care of the grading themselves, if they wanted the job done by a reasonable time. Many times they left the car at the end of the road and rode horses or the buckboard to the ranch house.

Lillie navigated between the frozen tracks, stopped at Hiram Two Hats to deliver the box, and finally reached the home lane. It sloped to the west and caught the afternoon sun. Thankfully, Fred kept the lane fairly smooth. She was glad because her arms ached from the rough road. She pulled through the open sliding door into the garage. She hopped out and grabbed the door to close it, but it was frozen to the ground. It had been that way for several weeks. She grumbled, "Why do I even try to shut this thing? It won't shut until spring, and then we won't need to shut it."

Fred was inside the kitchen when his bride of six months burst in the door. She dropped her bags of groceries on the table, ran to him, and gave him a big kiss.

"Honey, did you know there is a big Valentine's dance in two weeks?" Fred didn't say a word.

"I'd really like to go. Sid Carpenter and the Sawbucks are going to be there, and I know you like them."

Fred remained silent, but he turned and gave her a wink.

"Fred, you devil, you already know about it. Don't you?"

Fred finally spoke. "Yes, I bought two tickets. I'm thinking you will need a new dress for the occasion."

"Oh, Freddy, dear, you read my mind. As a matter of fact, Julie told me she is expecting a new shipment from Sioux Falls on Tuesday, and she was going to pick up one dress for me."

"Well, she better bring more dresses than that. I've never seen you satisfied with the first one."

On Tuesday, Lillie coaxed Fred to go to town with her. They stopped at the dress shop. Julie had picked the perfect dress for the occasion. It was red with silver sequins around the plunging neckline. It showed her bra in the middle. Fred let out a whistle when she tried it on.

"Don't you think it is cut a little low in front?" he asked.

"Not at all," answered Julie. "All the girls are wearing them this low. We have to show the men we are girls, after all."

Lillie looked at her husband. "Do you really think it shows too much of me?"

"Yes, but if you like it, buy it. I'll carry a baseball bat with me to fend off the single men," he said with a smile. "But I think you will need new shoes and a new coat to go with the outfit. You'd better buy some new underwear, too. That dress shows everything."

"Don't worry, Fred, I've got new foundations direct from Chicago. I have s everal new brassieres from Paris which dip below the cut. I've even got a little red one. You won't recognize Lillie when I get done with her," Julie cooed.

Lillie bought the red dress plus new shoes, a new coat with a fox fur collar, and leather gloves lined with rabbit fur. Fred told the pair he was going across the street to the café while Lillie bought her underwear. Lillie and Julie smiled and headed for the lingerie racks.

"Try this little number on, Lillie," said Julie as she held up a skimpy bra. "Wow! Are you sure this will hold everything in?"

"Sure, I'll help you adjust it. See, it has only one hook in the back. Hurry, get in the dressing room and let's see it on you."

Lillie slipped into the new brassiere. It felt as if she had nothing on.

"Don't I need a slip or something to hide my panty line and garters?"

"Gotcha! I'll be back in a minute."

She returned with a red slip, a red garter belt, and red panties.

"When Fred sees you in this, you won't be able to keep him away from your body. I better throw in a big stick, too."

Lillie replied, "You can forget the stick. I need a little loving."

"Well, have him be careful as he takes everything off. If you know what I mean."

Lillie bought everything. She couldn't wait to show Fred when they returned home. She threw her bundle in the back seat and ran to the café to get Fred. Once home, she ran upstairs and hung the dress.

"Do you want to see what I bought, honey?"

"Not right now, sugar. I've got to check the cows and see if Charlie fed them. He was taking off early."

Charlie was their hired hand, and single. He lived with Thoenes during the week and went home to St. Charles for the weekends.

"Is Sherry coming over tonight to be here for tomorrow's round-up? The cows will be calving in a month and they need to sorted for due dates."

"No, she had a date tonight, so she will be here early in the morning. She promised she wouldn't be late."

"So we are alone tonight?"

"Yep."

"I'll be in before six. You can show me after supper."

Fred hurried through his chores in anticipation of one of the few nights he and Lillie had alone. He entered the kitchen to find Lillie in a robe. The bathtub was in the middle of the room.

"Thought I'd take a bath after we eat. The only interruption I'll have is you. You will wash my back, won't you?"

"Sure, it will be my pleasure."

Fred loved to be alone with his wife once in a while. They had married in August. The honeymoon was short because of the wheat harvest. Lillie, although she was from South Dakota, jumped right in to feed the men and tolerated living with hired hands down the hall at night.

Lillie fried three hamburgers in the skillet and sliced some bread. She opened a can of corn and put a pan on for potatoes. The room grew warm. It would be just right for a bath. Fred set the table, then pumped some water from the cistern and placed it on the stove to heat.

After they finished supper, Lillie pulled the tub close to the big iron-footed cook stove. She tested the water with her elbow. It was hot, but not too hot. She signaled to her waiting husband. She was ready for her bath.

"Put a little cold in to start," she ordered.

She stripped off her robe and sat in the big tub. This would be quite a luxury. The room was warm. Fred had lit two kerosene lamps and turned off the dying electric light. He was trying to save the batteries in the basement. He dipped a sauce pan into the water and poured it over Lillie's head. She screamed at the shock of the extra warm water and threw up her arms to protect herself. The second pan wasn't quite as bad. Fred handed her the white bar of Ivory soap and washcloth, then continued to dump water on her body until the tub was half full. He grabbed the rag from her hand and scrubbed her smooth back. She bent forward and hugged her knees.

"Don't stop!" she whispered. "It feels so good."

Fred continued to wash and massage her back. He stopped and dipped in the pan for some more water. As he spilled the water over her back, she leaned back so the water would splash in her face and down her front. Fred made sure he poured on her chest. He grinned as the bubbles slid away from between her breasts and down her stomach. She reached up and grabbed Fred, pulled him to her lips, and kissed him.

"I love you, Fred Thoene. I love you with all my heart."

Fred couldn't help but steady himself by placing his hand on her breasts. They were slick, and his hand continued down her slim body to her crotch.

"Oops!" he said.

Lillie just smiled and adjusted his hand to her thigh.

"How about I give you a back wash?"

Fred didn't hesitate. "Sure, that would be great, but there isn't enough room for the both of us in the tub."

"I know, silly. Hand me a towel and I'll get out while you get undressed."

Fred handed his bride a warm towel and helped her up. He watched her dry as he stripped off his clothes. *She is lovely*, he thought. *She can't weigh over 120 pounds soaking wet. How did I ever get so lucky?*

He sat in the tub and waited. Lillie wrapped the towel around her body and began to pour water over her husband.

He sure is a handsome cowboy, all that dark wavy hair and curly chest hair. We're going to have a wonderful life together, she thought, mesmerized.

He gave her the soapy washrag for his back. She began to wash and massage at the same time. Her movements loosened her towel, and it fell open. She made a frantic grab, but it was too late. The towel fell on the floor. Lillie gave Fred a smirk. He glanced at her naked body and smiled. She kicked the towel to the side.

"It was a hindrance," she said with a giggle. "You're almost done anyway. Here's your towel. I'll throw down some clothes for you while I dress up in my new outfit."

Lillie hurried upstairs. She threw down jeans and a flannel shirt for Fred, but no underwear.

"Where's my long johns?" he called back upstairs.

"You won't need any after you see me. You'll be so hot for me, you'll be burning up."

Fred started to anticipate the coming evening. He pulled on his jeans and was careful zipping the fly. He half buttoned his shirt. He was just about to sit when he noticed the red light on the counter. It was a warning that the batteries for the lights were becoming low. He groaned before he looked out the window. In the light of the half-moon, he could see the windmill turning, the blades spinning in the constant South Dakota wind. He put on his shoes without socks and went down into the basement. In the semi-darkness, he could see the switch. He slammed the handle down. The bank of battery light started to blink. It would take all night to re-charge. Tonight it would be kerosene lanterns. He carried an extra lantern up the stairs and lit one. The room glowed golden. He sat down in his favorite chair and waited for Lillie.

He didn't have to wait long.

"Are you ready?" came a sweet voice from the hallway.

"You bet!"

Lillie entered the room in her new red coat with fur collar. She had her red hat pulled over her ears. Her brown hair peeked out beneath the upturned rim. She put her red-gloved finger to her lips and struck a sexy pose. She took one finger and flipped off her red knit hat. Then she slowly unbuttoned her coat and slipped it off. Fred whistled as she stood there in a slinky red dress with silver sequins flowing down from her shoulders. The low-cut bodice opened to the middle of her chest. She adjusted the dress to pull the front a little higher. She didn't want to expose her frilly underwear. The hemline at the bottom was almost mid-thigh. Fred scanned her up and down.

"You look terrific!" he exclaimed.

"You haven't seen it all," she replied.

"There's more?"

"You haven't seen the underneath."

"Okay, show me."

Lillie unzipped the side zipper that loosened the tight-fitting garment. She let the little cap sleeves slide from her shoulders. The dress made a red and sliver puddle on the floor. She stood for a second or two to let Fred's eyes follow the curves of her body. Then she grabbed the hem of the red slip and pulled it over her head. All she wore was her red panties and brassiere. She moved closer to her adoring husband. He grabbed her arm and pulled her down to his lap. With one hand he reached for a blanket beside him. It was one he used when he took a nap at noon. She cooed and embraced his neck. They kissed. It didn't take long for Fred to find the hook on the back of her bra. She unbuttoned his shirt and ran her fingers across his chest.

"I love you," she murmured.

"Let's go upstairs to bed, honey."

"Yeah, let's."

She slid from Fred's lap and gathered her discarded clothes. Fred picked up the lantern. He followed his bride upstairs. They crawled into bed naked and made passionate love.

The next thing Lillie heard was, "Mrs. Thoene, are you here?"

Lillie jerked awake. She leapt out of bed and threw on her robe. She ran to the top of the stairs and looked down. There was Sherry standing on the lower landing, looking up.

"Sorry, Sherry! Fred and I were out late last night and I guess we forgot to set the alarm. I'll be down in a minute. You can start peeling the potatoes. We have nine hungry men coming for dinner."

She dressed in her ordinary housedress and shook Fred.

"Fred, wake up. We overslept."

He rubbed his eyes and looked at the wind-up alarm clock. It read 7:30. He, too, leapt out of bed and dressed. Lillie was down in the kitchen first. She apologized again.

"It's alright, Mrs. Thoene. Everyone needs a good night's sleep," Sherry said with a slight smile. She knew her boss was fibbing. The couple had not gone anywhere, because she had called the evening before and Lillie told her they were staying home. They may have been out late, but they were not out of the house.

Fred emerged at the door. "Is Charlie here, too?"

"I think so, Mr. Thoene. Doesn't he drive a model T pick-up?"

"I'll skip breakfast, honey."

"No, you come back at eight and I'll have breakfast ready. Bring Charlie in, too."

Fred shook his head and hurried outside. He brought Charlie in at eight.

"How many men are actually coming?" asked Lillie.

"Let me see. There's Ken and Louie Stevens, Johnnie Wilkins, Hiram Two Hats, he asked if he could bring two of his friends because they need some money, Charlie, and me. That's eight. You might as well plan on Dad. He'll have to make sure we are doing it right."

"Okay, honey, Sherry and I will be ready."

Fred and Charlie returned outside.

Around ten, Julius and Olive, Fred's parents, arrived. Olive brought three freshly baked apple pies. She was always a big help in the kitchen. Julius headed for the feed yard and the rest of the cowboys.

At noon, the men entered the porch. Olive was there to meet them. She glared at the dirty boots and said, "No one comes in here with those filthy boots on. Leave them on the porch."

The men knew not to challenge Olive, so off came the boots. The two friends of Hiram's were embarrassed. Their socks had big holes in them. Fred didn't waste a minute. He hurried through the kitchen and upstairs. When he returned, he handed each a pair of new socks.

"Looks like you need these more than I do."

The two natives looked shocked at first, but readily accepted.

"Thank you very much, Mr. Thoene. We appreciate the kind gift. Any time you need help, you just tell Hiram. We come fast."

After a big dinner of meatloaf, potatoes, and corn, each man got a big slice of Olive's apple pie.

Hiram sat back in his chair and rubbed his belly.

"It will be difficult work after a meal like that. Thank you, Mrs. Thoene."

"You know Hiram, I think it is time you call me, Lillie. We plan on being neighbors for a long time."

"Okay, I'll try, Mrs. Thoene. Uh, Lillie."

*****

The two weeks passed quickly. Lillie didn't have much time to think about the big dance. The week finally arrived. As South Dakota weather goes, a southerly wind blew across the Plains, and the temperature rose to 50 degrees on Wednesday. Thursday was also very warm. The grass started to green. Friday brought rain and the mud road to Bonesteel become very soft. Lillie wondered if they could drive out to the dance on Saturday. The sky cleared for a short while, and Fred put on the tire chains to help navigate the mud road. He assured Lillie they would make it to the dance. He went as far as riding down the road on his horse and opening the gates to the several pastures. They would drive through the pasture if they had to.

Lillie started getting ready at four o'clock. She warmed plenty of water on the huge cook stove for her bath. She dragged out the large round wash tub and locked the doors. She didn't want any intruders barging in. She was dressed in her robe when Fred arrived at 5:30. He hurried through his bath and shaved. By 6, they were both ready to leave.

"Better take your galoshes, Lillie. It may be muddy in town. I wouldn't want you to get those red dancing shoes muddy," Fred told his lovely spouse.

Fred and Lillie literally plowed their way to Highway 18. Once they made the highway, Lillie commented, "That cloud bank to the north sure looks ominous. Are they predicting snow?"

"Yeah, I think maybe an inch or two, but you know accurate they are!"

Instead of stopping and removing the chains, Fred decided he'd just drive slowly. He'd need the chains to get back home. Once at the Odd Fellows Hall, they joined the crowd waiting inside. A supper was served first while the band set up. At eight, the floor was cleared and the band started to play. Fred and Lillie danced the Charleston, the Shimmie and, of course, what South Dakotan couldn't polka and schottische. Everyone was having a good time.

Very few noticed the wind picking up outside. By eight thirty, a monster storm was passing through the state. The temperature dropped twenty degrees in an hour. Snow began falling at a fast rate. The wind increased to forty miles per hour. Drifts quickly formed. Fred stepped outside to check. When he returned to their table, he commented, "Looks dangerous out there. We may have a tough time getting home."

During the break at ten, the mayor of Bonesteel stepped to the bandstand.

"I have just received a call from the South Dakota Highway Patrol. Outside there is a blizzard starting. They have closed Highway 18 west of Gregory. They recommend staying overnight in town or leaving immediately if you must get home."

Fred looked at Lillie. She already knew the answer. He had a hundred stock cows depending on his care. Fred would want to leave immediately. The pair said their good-byes and hurried outside. The snow fell with great intensity. There were five inches on the ground and more swirling around the few buildings in Bonesteel. The snow and wind increased once the pair reached the highway. The wind roared out of the northwest. The snow was blowing across the road. It was almost a white-out. Fred directed all the heat from the heater to the windshield. The wipers cleared away the snow but became encrusted with ice. Fred had to stop and beat the ice off with his fist. They drove slowly on the mostly abandoned road. Fred had to guide the car by watching the ridge of gravel on the side of the road. Lillie tried to spot the little sign which directed people to the Thoene Ranch.

"There it is," shouted Lillie.

Now it was only four miles to home. Fred turned down the narrow road. The mud had frozen into a series of ridges and ruts. The wind drove the snow across the frozen mud trail. Any place there was a small rise of the road bank, drifts were forming across the road. With the wind from the northwest, Fred could open his window to focus on the fence line. There were ditches on each side, but they were shallow. If he could stay to the middle, they would be all right.

The first mile gave them no problems. The second mile was more treacherous with the deeper cuts and larger drifts, but the Dodge seemed to take each drift in stride. Fred just gunned the motor and the car plowed through the drift. At times the snow was as high as the fender on the passenger side.

At mile three, they passed Hiram Two Hats' house. Fred could barely make out the outline of the small home in the darkness. There were no lights, but it was late.

They started the fourth mile, the most rolling. The drifts were growing. The wind rocked the car. Fred began climbing the last hill one half mile from the house. As he breached the hill, the lights shone into a cloud of white. Fred slowed, which proved a bad move. Ahead was a four-foot drift completely covering the road. The Dodge hit with a vengeance, but this one was too great. The front drove up and over the pile of snow and stopped.

Fred threw the car in reverse. It retreated a few feet. The chains churned at the frozen mud. The car wouldn't budge. Fred rocked the car back and forth until there was no movement at all.

Fred looked at Lillie and said, "Well, honey, I guess we'll have to hoof it from here."

"I'm glad I brought galoshes. At least I won't ruin my new shoes," Lillie answered.

Fred opened his door and stepped out into the howling storm. Lillie tried her door. It wouldn't move. She slid across the seat and exited out the driver's side. For a moment the two stood silently, looking at the task ahead. Fred took Lillie's hand and they climbed over the first snowbank. The wind tore at their coats. Lillie tied an old scarf from the car over her head. It would help keep her from losing her precious red hat. The snow was deep and it crept up underneath Lillie's red coat. The driving snow stung Lillie's almost bare legs. Three drifts later, they were both puffing.

"Can we stop for a break?" asked Lillie.

"No, we must press on."

Lillie stumbled and fell, tearing her new silk stockings. She skinned her knee.

"Please, Fred, let me stop," she pleaded.

He said nothing, but helped her up and pushed her ahead of him, trying to break the wind with his body. They finally made the lane. Now it was only a few hundred feet to go. Lillie fell again.

"You go ahead and turn the lights on and come back get me. I can't go any further," she whined.

"No!" was the scolding answer. Fred knew if they stopped, they would freeze to death. The wind chill had to be below zero. He prodded and coaxed. He grabbed his wife around her waist and pulled her ahead. He could see the back porch, just a few more steps.

They made the door. He turned the knob. A gust of wind grabbed the door and slammed it into the house, tearing the retaining spring from the frame. Fred dragged Lillie inside and with great effort he pulled the door shut and latched it. His fingers were so cold he could barely move them. He opened the door to the house and grabbed Lillie's coat collar. He pulled his frozen spouse inside the kitchen and sat her on a chair.

He flicked on the light. The single bulb was dim. The batteries must be getting low again. In the semi-darkness he found two kerosene lamps. His fingers were so cold he had to struggle to open the match box. He turned the wick higher to get more light. So what if he had to replace the wicks tomorrow? This was a critical time. He had to get his mind into a survival mode.

What next? he thought. *Light the stove, get into dry clothes, find a blanket for Lillie.*

He stumbled into the spare bedroom next to the kitchen. It was then he realized he had lost a shoe. His feet were so cold he didn't realize it was missing. He kicked off the other as he grabbed the bedspread from the bed. He returned to Lillie and wrapped her as best he could. She was shivering out of control. He had to hurry.

He gathered some firewood from the porch and shoved it into the firebox of the stove. Next he crumpled some newspaper and threw it in. Finally, he got a measuring cup and poured a cup full of kerosene on the wood. He grabbed a match and struck it on the side of the stove, then lit the fuel. The fire leapt to life. Soon it was roaring and producing heat.

Fred hurried upstairs and changed out of his wet suit into a pair of dungarees and a heavy flannel shirt. He grabbed Lillie's flannel pajamas and some wool socks. He found Lillie slumped over the table. He pushed her shoulders back and slapped her face. She snapped awake and glared at him.

"Damm you! You go to hell, Fred Thoene!" she screamed.

Fred smiled. His wife was going to be okay. He picked her up and sat her on the table and unbuttoned her coat. Holding her up with one arm, he unzipped her red dress. He worked from her shoulders and to the floor. She shivered in her slip as he sat down again.

"Hang on, honey, I'll heat some water for your feet."

He wrapped her up again and headed for the cistern pump. He pumped a large kettle of water and set it on the burners. Next he dipped the coffee pot into the drinking water pail. He knew Lillie needed and liked hot black coffee. It was the Swede in her.

While the water heated, he returned to his shivering wife. He had to get those tattered silk hose off. He spun her sideways and raised her slip high to unsnap the hooks on her garter belt, then slid her stockings down her legs. She smiled slightly. Fred rounded up the foot tub and placed her feet in it. He tested the water on the stove with his elbow. It was warm but not hot. He poured in the pail. Next he poured some of the hot water into a pair of hot water bottles and tucked them inside Lillie's blanket. He poured her some coffee. It warmed her from the inside.

The old clock chimed two times in the hall. Fred finally sat down. He changed the water in the bucket and placed his feet in with Lillie's. They played footsie for a couple of minutes.

Lillie spoke. "Do you think we could lie down now?"

"Yes, I think we are safe. I brought your pajamas down and laid them by the stove. They should be warm."

Lillie stood and steadied herself with the table. Her feet were still numb.

"I don't think I can walk that far. Can you get them?"

"Sure."

Lillie leaned against the table and pulled her slip over her head. When Fred turned around she was struggling with her brassiere. Her fingers still weren't functioning well. Fred helped her unhook the garment and handed her the top of her pajamas. The warm fabric felt wonderful. She quickly sat and pulled on her bottoms. Fred helped with the heavy wool socks. She headed for the sofa across the room and motioned with her finger for Fred to follow. He turned the damper down on the stove pipe to slow the burning of the wood. They lay down together and fell asleep.

They were awakened by a knocking on the door.

"Fred, Lillie, are you all right? It's me, Hiram Two Hats. I saw your car in the road and hurried over, hoping you made it to the house."

"Yes, we're okay, Hiram. Come on in."

Hiram entered the kitchen and viewed the mess. There were clothes lying all over, puddles of water on the floor, and two empty coffee cups on the table.

The grizzled old neighbor shook his head and said, "You're lucky to be alive. We had a full-blown blizzard last night. There is about twelve inches of snow and it is twelve below."

Fred struggled to rise. His knees wobbled. He grabbed the table and pulled out a chair. Lillie sat up and blinked her eyes. Hiram smiled. It was then Lillie realized she was still in her pajamas and the front was open because their fingers last night were too cold to button them. She quickly pulled the blanket up around her.

"I know," said Fred, "and we are thankful for neighbors who care. How about some coffee?"

The next minute there was another knock on the door. It was Charlie. He had ridden nine miles on horseback to check on his boss. Charlie had a girlfriend, but she lived in Fairfax, ten miles away. He was going to see her this weekend, but his old pickup broke down and he had to stay in Bonesteel. He borrowed a horse from a friend and rode out to the ranch to make sure everything was okay. It had been a cold ride, but he was warmly dressed. All they could see was his eyes when he stepped in.

"I saw your car in the middle of the road, then I found this shoe at the end of the lane. I was hoping I would find you and the missus here and not in the middle of the lane. Are you okay?" Charlie asked.

"Yes, we're okay now, but there a couple of times I thought we might freeze to death. We definitely weren't dressed for a hike."

"Well, you don't worry, Boss. I'll put Zinger in the barn and check the cattle. If I find any trouble, I'll come back in."

Lillie replied, "You take Hiram with you and I'll have hot coffee and pancakes for you when you return."

As soon as the two men left, Lillie burst out laughing.

"What's so funny?"

"Didn't you see the look on Hiram's face when I sat up? I was unbuttoned down to my waist. I'm sure he got his eyes full. Wait until he gets home and tells Rosey."

"Well, I think he has seen a woman's bosom before."

"Maybe, but not mine!"

Out the window, Lillie watched the two men trudging through snow to the barns. It was safe to leave the kitchen and get properly dressed. Fred followed her upstairs.

Hiram and Charlie had to dig their way to the building. Some drifts were eight feet high. Charlie led Zinger inside and fed him some hay. They found the cattle to be fine. Fred's dad was smart in building to face south. It protected the cows from the howling north winds. Although the snow was piled high, the cattle withstood the blizzard.

After a big breakfast, Fred decided he was warm enough to venture out. He and Hiram rode their horses to the stuck Dodge. They determined tomorrow would be a better day to extract the car from the snowbank. It would take some digging, for all they could see was the top half of the vehicle. Fred scheduled a time with Hiram to come help. He and Charlie would bring a team of horses to pull the car out backwards.

Fred and Charlie worked the rest of the afternoon, making the cows as comfortable as possible. They headed inside around four. Lillie had recovered also and was baking some fresh bread.

The next morning the wind was calm, but it was twelve below zero again. Fred and Charlie had breakfast and dressed for the cold.

"We'll be back in close to noon, honey. Maybe if we get the car out we can stay in the rest of the day."

After checking and feeding the cows, they hitched up the team. Fred rode his horse and Charlie rode astride one of the team. They rode out through the pasture, staying to the top of the ridges to avoid the drifts. It took about a mile of maneuvering to go the half mile to the stuck auto.

They met Hiram at the Dodge. First they dug the snow away from the back of the car, then up to the driver's side door. Charlie hitched the team to the Dodge. Fred got in and put the shifter in neutral. Horses are strong, but pulling against the motor was unnecessary. Fred stuck his arm out the window and signaled. "Let's go."

With a mighty pull, the team strained at the harness. The car budged, then popped out of the snowbank like a cork from a bottle of wine. They tugged it backwards for about a hundred feet. Fred and Hiram dug the packed snow from beneath the fenders. Fred got in and hit the starter. All he got was a groan.

"Bring the team around front, Charlie. Maybe we can start this machine by pulling it. I'll put it in road gear to get the motor to turn over. I've only got 10 weight oil in the engine."

Charlie drove the team around front. Hiram hooked the pulling tree. Charlie let out a "Hee, haw!" and the team jerked forward. About two turns of the tires, and the engine caught fire. There were a couple of pops out the exhaust and she purred like a kitten.

Fred let the car warm up some, then got out.

"Thank you for helping out, Hiram. Tell Rosey hi. Charlie, if I can turn this Dodge around, I'll follow you through the pasture. The team can break the drifts better than this car."

Getting home was not too difficult. The car only got stuck once. Luckily, the team was ready and pulled the Dodge through. When they got back into the house at one, they were cold and hungry. They shed their outerwear in the porch and headed inside. Lillie had been busy. The kitchen was warm and smelled of fresh cookies and cake.
It wasn't long after dinner, their main midday meal, that the long night and busy morning caught up with Fred, Lillie, and Charlie. Fred fell asleep in his chair; Charlie stretched out on the couch, and Lillie went into Sherry's room and laid on her bed. They all had a nice nap.

The sun was setting when Fred awoke. He slipped out for a quick check of the livestock. Everyone was fine. They ate a leftover supper and spent the rest of the evening playing Parcheesi. Tomorrow would be a nicer day. This was South Dakota, after all.

Ten Tin Cans

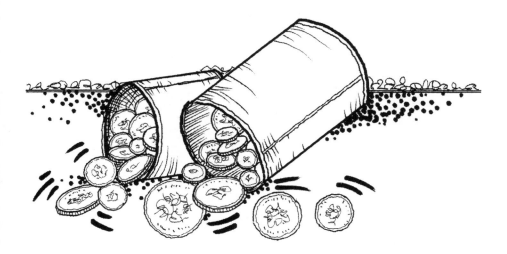

Harold Dubachek died peacefully in his sleep. It was an apparent heart attack. He was a very rich man and a long-time member of St. James Christian Church of Toledo. At the funeral services, Pastor Ted Williams praised Mr. Dubachek for his many gifts and talents he had given to the congregation. Secretly, Pastor Ted also anticipated a large contribution to the building fund from Harold Dubachek's estate. Pastor anticipated overseeing the building of a new sanctuary which might advance his position within the church.

On the day after the funeral, Harold's lawyer called the church and asked if Ted and the board chairman could meet in his office, because the church was to receive a bequest.

Doing his best to contain his excitement, Ted called Charlie Sneed, the board chairman. "Charlie, guess what? Harold Dubachek's lawyer just called. He would like us to meet him in his office. There's an unusual bequest in his will. Can we go this afternoon?"

"Well, if he can wait until three, we can. I have two appointments after lunch."

"The lawyer said he would be there all afternoon, so I'll call and let him know.

You know the place, right? Landus, Smith, & Howe, at the First National Bank Building. See you at three."

At two forty- five, Ted met Charlie in the bank lobby. Together they rode the elevator to the fourth floor.

"This is going to be a great day for our church," Ted said proudly.

"I wouldn't count my chickens before they are hatched," Charlie warned.

Ted gave Charlie a sly smile as they entered Mr. Landus' office. Harold's three children were there. Everybody exchanged pleasantries and sat down.

Mr. Landus explained the procedure of Harold's last will and testament. All parties were present at the meeting, except one.

"Does anyone here know of a Bob Thoen?"

"Who?" asked Charlie

"Robert Thoen. We found some family living in Columbus, Nebraska, some in Lyle, Minnesota, and one family on a ranch near Winner, South Dakota. None of them matched the description in the will."

Charlie smiled and asked, "How are you spelling that name?"

"T-H-O-E-N. Isn't that right?"

Charlie looked at the young lawyer sitting across from him. "Try adding an 'E' after the name. T-H-O-E-N-E. Since I can tell you haven't experienced the German surnames to a great degree, that name is pronounced 'Tay- nee.' I know a Robert Thoene very well. I think he was a member of our church a long while back." Charlie said, "He and his wife left just after you came, Pastor Ted. He was a quiet person. I don't know if he had any family. I have no clue where he is now."

"Well, we haven't done much research," Mr. Landus said. "I'm sure we'll find him. It is significant for the church's part. It seems Bob has the key to the puzzle."

Charlie's face brightened. "You know, Vera Notting used to keep in touch with Bob's wife, Irma. I bet she knows where he is."

"That'll be fine. Can you let me know by next Monday?"

"Why is Bob so important?" asked Pastor Ted.

"There are several properties and financial instruments not yet accounted for. According to his will, they seem to be connected to ten tin containers hidden in Mr. Dubachek's house. Mr. Thoene apparently worked for Harold when he built the house. According to the will, he was hired by Mr. Dubachek to build the hiding places for the containers. Unless we find Mr. Thoene, we cannot dispense the entire estate. He holds the key. If he cannot be found, the house will be sold and the contents."

"Do you think there'll be money for the church?" Ted asked.

"No one knows. Harold Dubachek was a generous man. We can only assume. Right?"

Ted constrained his smile, doing his best not to appear eager. "This is truly a mystery, but one I think can be easily solved. I'll help Charlie find Mr. Thoene right away."

He turned toward Charlie and said, "Well, Charlie, I guess we will have a busy weekend for our church. Won't we?"

"Call me if you have the right man, Mr. Sneed. The sooner we can contact Mr. Thoene, the better."

The meeting ended with all parties speculating on what Harold had stored inside those ten tin cans. Harold's children rode with them. Ted didn't say a word to Charlie while on the elevator. When they reached the ground floor, Tom Dubachek asked Ted what he thought of the will's stipulations.

"I don't know, but they are very interesting," Ted answered. "I guess we will know more after we find Mr. Thoene."

"Bob Thoene used to work on Saturdays and evenings for Dad. I figured it was none of my business as long as it didn't affect the firm. Mr. Thoene was the best finish man we ever had."

Worry showed on Tom's face. "I hope Bob is still alive. We would like to sell Dad's house. If we don't find the hiding places, the cans will go with the house."

"I'm sure we will find him." Ted spoke with a confident tone. "God will help us. He blessed Harold with great wealth. I don't think he will let this mystery go unsolved."

The next day, Pastor Ted called Vera. "Do you know where Bob Thoene is?"

"Sure do. He lives in Briggsville. I talk to his wife, Irma, all the time. He's doing fine. Why? "

Ted explained the stipulations in Harold's will and how Bob was important in solving the puzzle.

"You can call him yourself. I'm sure he'll remember you. I don't see any reason he wouldn't be willing to help. Boy, that old Harold was a sly one, wasn't he? He hid a bunch of tin cans in his house. Do they hold the clues to how much the church gets?"

"It could be a big chunk of money."

"You'd better not count your chickens before they're hatched," Vera warned.

"That's what Charlie told me. I'll call the lawyer right now. He wants to make the first contact."

Fifteen minutes after Ted called Mr. Landus, he had Bob on the phone.

"This is John Landus from Toledo. The reason I'm calling is that Harold Dubachek passed away last week. He left an inheritance for the church and you in ten tin containers. The will says very clearly you are the only person who knows where those cans are hidden. Is that correct?"

"First, I'm so sorry to hear of Harold's death. My sympathies to his family. Yep, that's right. When I worked for Mr. Dubachek, he had me build several hidden cabinets. I remember the first one. He had me put notes with a code for the others. They will tell about the other sites. Three years ago, he asked me to help him place some containers in those cabinets. I sealed the containers and placed the first three in one of the pillars on the stairs. Two weeks later I placed two more cans, and in four weeks after that another two. He never called me again. I don't recall hiding the last three cans. He never told me what was inside the cans. I promised not to look. I had forgotten about those containers."

"Would you help us find the containers?"

"I will, if that was part of his bequest. Harold was a good man to work for."

The following Wednesday, Bob, the attorneys, Tom Dubachek, and Pastor Ted met at Harold's house. Tom unlocked the house. Bob brought his tool bag. Everyone went inside and Bob went straight for the staircase. He climbed to the second landing and set down his tools. He carefully scored the varnish around the knurl on the top of the bottom post. He wrapped it with an old washcloth and placed his largest pump pliers on the ball. With a strong jerk, the ball turned to the right and loosened.

The post was hollow. It held the first three cans. Taped on the last can was the message "4shel2tlib".

Bob studied the piece of paper. "Fourth shelf, second tier in the library," he told them. "I remember building it. Let's see what it holds. Tom, I'll need a stepladder. I think there is one in the garage."

Bob removed the books from the second shelf and handed them down to Tom. He also removed the books on the third shelf. Behind each shelf were two screws holding a piece of paneling which concealed a small cabinet containing two more cans. On the last can was taped another message. "3stpdnbckstr."

Tom said, "It sounds like it is in some staircase somewhere."

"Third step down from top, back stair," Bob said.

They rushed to the back stairs leading to the family room in the basement. Bob counted down three steps. He examined the step and fit a pry bar into a slot cut in the step's molding. Carefully, he pried off the quarter round. Behind the piece were two brass screws which he removed. The riser slipped down and revealed two more containers. Bob placed them into the box. On the last can out of little box was inscribed "4brkup3in2frpl."

This time Charlie was getting the feel of the codes. "Fourth brick up, third brick in second fireplace. But which one is the second fireplace?"

"It is in the den. Dad always called that one number two," Tom answered.

Sure enough, the brick there was a little loose. Bob could pry it out with two screwdrivers.

"That is eight. You said there are ten. I don't see any writing on the container," said Bob. "Maybe it fell off. Does someone have a flashlight?"

Bob almost crawled into the fireplace. He shot the light in the hole. There against the second layer of bricks was a stainless steel tube. He took a pair of pliers and lifted the tube out. On the outside was written, "Open immediately."

Bob screwed the cap off. Inside was a piece of paper. The heat had discolored it some. Bob handed it to Tom. Tom held it up to the light. It read "Nx1undntstdbdrmlft ld."

They wrote it down on a separate piece of paper and studied the code. Last one under nightstand bedroom lift lid.

When they got to the bedroom, they found the nightstand all right, but the lid didn't come off. Pastor Ted wiggled the table. It moved. The small scrap of carpet underneath also moved. There was a trap door. It had a recessed handle embedded in the lid. Ted lifted the small door. There was the ninth can. It had a piece of paper taped on it. "Lst1ontpshlpan."

"I've got that one," Ted shouted. "Last one on the top shelf in the pantry."

They carried the ladder into the pantry and Tom climbed up. There it was, sitting in plain view.

Bob chuckled. "Evidently, he didn't have time to hide this one."

Now they had all ten tin cans. "The will states the church picks the first can. Then Bob picks number two. They each alternate until all have been opened. Pastor Ted, you have the honor of first pick."

Ted reached for the first can. Bob handed him a screwdriver to open the top. It was empty except for the letter 'F'. Also inside was a piece of paper. It read, "This is for the many times you and this congregation saw a stranger and did nothing to welcome them. It says in the Bible, Matthew 25:43, 'I was a stranger and you did not invite me in.' Bob was one of those people. You greeted him as he walked in the door, but later everyone gathered into their little cliques to gossip, point fingers, and ignore him. After a year of trying, he came to me one afternoon after work and told me he was going to look elsewhere for a church. I didn't blame him one bit. We as a church failed. HD."

Bob chose the second container. He slowly opened the lid. Inside were a key and a note.

It read, "Bob, you have been a loyal and honest worker. I know you have helped many people without pay. For your efforts, you will find this key is for the cabin on the lake in Minnesota. Enjoy it. HD."

Ted picked up the third can and popped open the lid. Inside was another note from Harold. It read, "Another container that reflects our congregation's faults. Mary and I gave much of our time and money to the youth programs. We gave a substantial sum to build a new addition for Christian Education. It started out fine, but soon lost its luster. The adults forgot the young people and returned to their selfish ways. Have Bible classes when we want them, have church services when we want to attend, and for goodness sakes, get those noisy children out of the sanctuary during worship service, they demanded. In Luke 18:16, Jesus said, 'Let the little children come to me and do not hinder them, for the Kingdom of God belongs to such as these.' I give you an empty can. HD."

Bob took his turn and opened the fourth container. Inside was a certificate for one thousand shares of Eccon Oil. Attached to it was a note. Tears welled up in his eyes as he read it out loud. "I have given these shares to your church for whatever they might want to do with them. No strings attached. I know your congregation has several projects in the works and the only thing missing is money. Use it with God's blessing. HD."

Pastor Ted saw a pattern in the order of the cans. Instead of choosing the fifth tin, he went for the sixth. When he picked it up, it rattled. Eagerly, he opened it. Inside was a set of keys and a note.

Ted saw what it said and read it with a touch of disgust in his voice. "Ted, I have known you for ten years. I've tried to work with you, but you only look out for yourself. I know you have been anticipating my demise. You are planning big things with my money. Improvements to the building, a new sanctuary, maybe an associate minister were all on your agenda. All these projects were to build up your résumé for more important positions in our denomination. Instead of giving what you think the church should receive, I am giving you the keys to my Mercedes. Maybe you will not be able to advance as quickly as you would like, but now you can drive in style. HD."

Bob chose the fifth tin and opened it. Inside was a deed to a house in one of the many additions started by Dubachek Construction. The deed was made out to Bob and his wife. The note read, "This was a demonstration house that needs a little fixing. Bob, I hope you and your pretty wife can spend many years living there and enjoying your retirement. HD."

Ted was becoming noticeably irritated. He grabbed the eighth can and muttered something under his breath as he tore open the lid.

"Is there something you would like to say, Pastor?" asked Mr. Landus with a sly smile. He knew the pastor was not receiving what he expected.

"No," answered Ted brusquely.

When he read the note, he looked around the room. Was this some kind of a joke? It was as if Harold were watching.

The note read, "Ted, why did you take the eighth container instead the seventh? Did you think there would be extra in Bob's can? Are you still looking for that big check? You will not find the money you so greatly desired. I did leave the church some of my fortune. God has been good to me and I feel I should give back to Him part of my wealth. I have set up a trust fund to be distributed at a later date. The church will receive the interest and profits from the trust each year. This should amount to approximately $25,000 per year. Mary and I still love this old church and our many friends there. We hope this fund will sustain our church for a long while. Please use it with God's blessing. HD."

Bob cautiously opened the lid to the seventh container. The note read, "Bob, I know you and Irma have a special place in your hearts for the St. Jude Hospital. They saved your grandchild along with many prayers, I assume. I have instructed Mr. Landus to write a check in your name for one million dollars and give it to St. Jude's."

Pastor Ted sighed. His wonderful sanctuary was history. He picked up the ninth can and opened it. He was afraid of what he would find. The note read, "Pastor Ted, I know by now you are disappointed. You expected to receive big dollars from my estate. I have told you my reasons. It is humbling to not get what you anticipated. I will not leave you high and dry. Upon your retirement, a trust will be released and you will be comfortably provided for the rest of your life. God bless you, Pastor Ted."

Everyone in the room was anxious to see what the last container had in it. When Bob opened the can, he revealed that it was packed to the top with crumpled dollar bills. Bob took each bill and smoothed it out. When he got to the bottom, on the last dollar was written, "Go to the mantel and get the large black vase. Look inside."

Bob went into the den and retrieved the vase. He looked inside. There was a paper taped to the inside lip. It said, "Carefully wash the inside. It is just mud. Put through a sieve and the contents are yours. HD."

Bob poured water inside and loosened the mud. He swirled it around to mix up the contents. Slowly he poured the contents through a sieve. A large stone fell out. It was an uncut diamond. Bob washed the gem off and held it up. It sparkled in the sunlight.

Tom exclaimed, "That must be the diamond Dad always said he had. I never saw it before today. He claimed it was several carats in weight. It was worth thousands."

Bob turned to Tom and said, "Then it must be for you, not me. I could never accept such a valuable gift."

"No, no, it's yours. Don't you see? The pastor was supposed to pick up this can. He thought the last can contained the most valuable gift. He was wrong. His greed made him pick up the ninth can. Dad knew he would. Take and use it for your own needs. May I suggest a ring for Irma and the leftover be sold and invested in your retirement account."

"I have a better idea," said Bob. "I will have a jeweler craft a ring for my

Irma, because she never had an engagement ring. The remaining stone I will sell and give to the House of Love for homeless people."

"But you can't just give away money like that," sputtered Pastor Ted.

"And why not?" Bob quizzed him.

"Because they will just squander it and spend it on the poor and lonely."

"You'd suggest I'd give it to your church. They would hide it in a bank and not use it at all. You want to be like the servant who received his talent and buried it. No, that is not right. There may be one person who needs help. That person may find Jesus. He may be saved. Isn't that more important than money in a bank?"

Ted looked at Bob and said nothing. He knew he had been wrong. He had been on the wrong path for a long time. Maybe Harold was trying to open his eyes to his sins.

With tears in his eyes, Ted turned to Bob. "You are right. I have been selfish. I took a vow when I became a minister to tell people about Jesus and His love. I was to follow His teachings. I have failed. Bob, I need your strength to help me. Will you forgive me?"

"No, I'm not the one to give forgiveness, only Jesus can do that. You have found your way and strength again today. You pray to Him alone. I'm sure he will listen. Now go in peace."

The meeting was over. Everyone left the old Dubachek house. Everyone knew, even the lawyer, Harold had gotten what he wanted. His best employee was set for the rest of his life, his children were well taken care of because of his large estate, and, most importantly, he had returned his church and his pastor to Jesus.

Secret Codes
1. 4shel2tlib
2. 3stpdnbckstr
3. 4brkup3in2frpl
4. Nxundrntstdlftld
5. Lstiontpshfpan

Free Ride

"Hello, R and P Consultants. Pete Lester speaking."

"Mr. Lester, this is Heather Huseman from the Small Business Administration."

Pete paused before answering. "May I be of help to you, Miss Huseman? Or is it Mrs.?"

"Miss. I'm calling on behalf of the SBA because the General Accounting Office or GAO suspects fraudulent practices with a company in Iowa. We of the SBA can find no problems. We would like to contract a private firm like yours to investigate the company."

"I'm afraid we'd need more information before we would take on such a task," Pete said.

"I understand. Is there a possibility we could meet and discuss the full situation? I have authorization to come to your office and discuss this in detail."

"In that case, by all means. When can you meet with us?"

"Is sometime next week too soon?"

"No. How about Tuesday at 10 o'clock in the morning?"

"Sounds fine. I'll get my assistant to check for flights to Des Moines. See you then."

Pete hung the phone up and hurried into Ron's office.

"Hey, Ron, you'll never believe who I just made an appointment with," Pete blurted out.

"No, I probably wouldn't."

"A Miss Heather Huseman from the SBA wants to talk to us about investigating some business here in Iowa. She claims the GAO suspects fraud, but can't prove it. They want us to help. She is coming next Tuesday to explain the situation."

Ron White and Pete Lester were high school buddies and the most unlikely pair you could see together. Ron was tall and slim, whereas Pete was only 5'8" and one would say portly. They were not athletes or nerds. They both chose the music department of the high school. Each young man knew music would not be their final career, but music would be with them forever. After graduation, the relationship continued through college, although Ron went to State for an engineering degree. Pete attended an out-of-state university and majored in business administration. After college, they both bounced around from job to job but kept in touch, each searching for a better opportunity.

After being apart for several years, they met at a New Year's Eve party. They compared notes and found out both had the uncanny ability to analyze poor performing companies. Ron, with his analytical mind for details and solutions, could solve companies' problems. Pete understood the mechanics of bookkeeping and analysis of operation on the financial side. Before the night was over, they decided to start a business in which they would buy faltering companies, sell off divisions which were underperforming, then resell the new profitable firm.

The two men became quite wealthy, but the excitement wore off. The travel and long stays away from home taxed their families. The partnership of White and Lester dissolved and became R&P Business Consultants. They could work from a small hometown office, travel less, and because of their expertise, they were in high demand.

Tuesday morning arrived. Ron helped their office assistant, Ruby, set up the conference room. He wanted plenty of coffee and snacks available. He knew Ruby would be ready. She was a divorcée and very dependable. He had no idea of the length or breadth of the proceedings.

Miss Huseman arrived at precisely 10 o'clock. She was a thin woman with dark brown hair, standing close to six feet tall in her high heels. She was smartly dressed in a wine-red suit and white oxford cloth blouse. An assistant trailed behind her, loaded with files. The poor assistant was significantly shorter, with auburn hair that covered her head like a Brillo pad. She sighed as she plopped the folders on the table. She stood there bracing herself with her arms and took a deep breath, then released a puff of air upward to move a wayward strand out of her eyes.

"Karen is my right arm," announced the tall, thin, dark-haired woman, "and I am Heather Huseman, agent for the SBA."

Pete piped up, "This is my partner, Ron White, and I am Pete Lester. "

He pointed at Ruby and continued, "And this is our right-hand person, Ruby. Please have a seat. Would you like some coffee or tea?"

"Yes, I'd like some tea. What about you, Karen?" Heather replied.

"Do you have some iced tea?" asked Karen.

"You bet," answered Ruby, "The refrigerator is full. Sweet or unsweetened?"

"Unsweetened."

After a few minutes of pleasantries, Pete asked the big question. "What brings you to us, Miss Huseman?"

Heather unloaded the files Karen had placed on the desk.

She sighed and started. "There is a company named Airliner Corks and, in fact, it has a companion company named Riverton Recycling. Both are located in Riverton, Iowa. They have grants from the government for job creation, Housing and Urban Development, Office of Safety Health Administration, OSHA, Resource Enhancement and Protection, REAP, Employment and Training Agency, ETA, Federal Food and Drug, FDA, Fish and Wildlife Bureau, and several others from the State of Iowa.

"They also have a grant from a bill passed by the U.S. Congress giving them exclusive rights to a product they manufacture. Congressman Joel Hanover had an attachment to the Gun Control Bill to ensure their exclusive rights. You see, the town is in his district and had high unemployment. One of his campaign promises was for new jobs. He carried through. This bill opened a

Pandora's Box. The town soon found there were all kinds of money available through the federal government and state government. They hired a person to write and apply for all kinds of grants. They have been very successful.

"The problem is, we would like to know how they are using the money. Our investigation indicates nothing is shipped out of town, and very little is shipped in. The unemployment rate is below the state average of 4%. The two companies involved have not violated any rules and are on time with their loan payments."

"So what is your problem? Sounds like a solid plan to me," commented Pete.

"It isn't so much what they are doing wrong. We would like to know how they are accomplishing their goals. Are they manipulating their books? Are they cheating on their reporting of taxes? We'd like to know, but without just cause, we are not allowed to investigate. The courts would never allow a court order for this reason. Congressman Hanover would call for an investigation of the SBA if he found out. The SBA would like to contract your firm to go to Riverton under the guise of possibly purchasing the companies or maybe act as investigating reporters for a business magazine. You would be compensated on a per diem basis directly from the GAO office. There will be no connection to the SBA or any other involved agency."

"Sounds like an interesting job. What about travel expenses?"

"Oh, I have vouchers for you. I promise every expense will be covered. I cannot promise any bonuses or extra pay, but when finished, any non-sensitive material may be used for your benefit."

Ron turned to Pete and asked, "What do think, Pete?"

Pete's face was all smiles.

"This sounds like a lot of fun. We've never worked on a government project before. Why not? I'd like to know more about this town, too. While you and Heather were talking, I located Riverton. It is located on the Des Moines River in southern Iowa, only 75 miles away. There would be very few nights away from home. I doubt if there are any motels in town. I would like to know what it is these two companies manufacture?"

"Good question." answered Miss Huseman. "The Airliner Company has the patent for remanufactured corks to be used exclusively in wine bottles. They somehow recycle used wine bottle corks for use again. The Riverton Recycling is a little more elusive. We know they receive product from Airliner, but what they do after that is not documented."

"So we would have to investigate the product itself and the plant before we could develop an analysis."

"That is probably a good plan."

"Well, what do you think, Ron?"

"It sounds exciting to me. I say we try it."

"Great! I agree," replied Pete.

"I have the contract with me," Heather said. "You can sign it and I'll be on my way. I'll expect a report once a month, but, of course, all reports will be sent through the GAO."

Ron and Pete signed the contract. They helped Heather and Karen load the voluminous files into their car and shook hands.

"I wish you two the best of luck and I'll be anxious to hear your analysis," Heather said as she slid into the driver's seat. She adjusted her skirt, which had crept up to mid-thigh. "See you gentlemen later."

She started the auto, gave the two men a sweet smile, and the two women left.

Ron turned to Pete. "It's a good thing our wives weren't here. Those two women were really babes."

"Yeah, that Heather was smoking hot. How did she land a government job?"

Both men grinned, then were snapped back into reality by the ever-present Ruby.

"You'd better get your heads out of the clouds. We've got a lot of work to do." She warned, "Also, I ran Miss Hot Stuff through the computer. She's the daughter of a friend of the senator from Iowa. She's well-educated, with a MBA degree from Harvard. She has two brothers, drives BMWs, likes Coors beer, wears designer dresses, and hangs out in Bermuda."

"Boy, Rube, you didn't miss much."

"I just didn't want you boys to get too excited and get in trouble with your wives."

Ron and Pete turned toward Ruby. Their older office assistant always brought them back to earth. Ruby had seen some bad times now and then, so she was always practical. She treated her younger bosses as her sons.

They let her mother them. Their wives also liked Ruby. They knew she would keep the partners on the straight and narrow.

"Okay, Rube, crank up the old computer. See what you can dig up on these two wayward companies."

Within the hour, Ruby appeared with information on Airliner Corks and Riverton Recycling.

"There is quite a bit on Airliner, but very little on Riverton Recycling. It seems the cork factory owner invented a way to recycle old wine bottle corks by grinding them into dust, then reforming them with the help of a resin-like material. In the re-manufacturing process, a metal wedge was embedded in the cork. This is linked to a T-shaped handle which makes it possible to remove the stopper without the need for a cork remover. It made the removal of the cork much easier. For a while, they had the market for many of the airlines. He also had exclusive rights to all the U.S. Congress eating areas, thanks to Congressman Joel Hanover's efforts.

"As for the recycling plant, all I could find out is that it is a subsidiary of Airliner Cork and it loses money every year. They made a cork brick for playgrounds, but it looks as if the market for the bricks has vanished. It doesn't give a reason for the decline. However, the company still is functioning and hires 30 employees. I suggest a visit to the plant to find out more information," Ruby reported.

"But how do we get in the door? We can't just barge in and say, 'We would like to see your books,'" said Ron.

"And we can't pretend we are some kind of reporters, as Miss Hot Stuff suggested," added Pete., "Anybody there could check on us and find out we are a bogus pair."

"We need another angle."

"I wish we were still in the buying and selling business."

"Bingo! You said a mouthful. That's what we have to do."

"What's that?"

"Resurrect our old company. That's what. Ruby, do we still have some old stationery?"

"Yes, we have some left in the closet. I've been using it for scratch paper."

"Do we still have the old website?"

"We still own the website, but we haven't used it for several years. I can see if we can reactivate the site."

"Good. If we have a website, we will look legit."

It took three days to launch their website. They changed the name on the door to include White & Lester, Inc. The second weekend, Pete and family decided on a family outing in and around Riverton. The children, Emma and Jodi, were not very excited about the adventure until they passed several horse and buggies. They were intrigued with the many barefooted children and steel-wheeled tractors. Riverton was on the edge of Amish country.

The family drove around town, hoping not to look too much like outsiders. Turning to the small downtown area, Amy, Pete's wife, spotted a general store. It was time to go shopping. The store was full of bulk items, homemade pies, and yards and yards of fabric. While the girls investigated the large store, Pete walked two blocks west of the downtown to the large metal building he surmised was the Airliner Cork Works.

The building was actually two separate buildings connected by several cross corridors. As is in many small Iowa towns, the streets were just tar and gravel. The only paved street was Main Street and the short branch to Airliner. Pete could see the office was just a couple of rooms in front. The rest of the building must be manufacturing, he thought. Pete walked around the entire complex, which covered the entire block. The grounds were well-manicured. He returned to the downtown and found his family, loaded with packages, waiting at the car.

"There's an ice cream shop inside, Daddy. May we have a cone? Mommy said we had to wait until you got back."

Pete looked at Amy and winked. "Sounds like a good idea. Is it going to be one dip or two?"

"I think two dips, but in a dish," Amy suggested.

"Okay, let's go back in, then we head for home."

"I saw a poster for a restaurant in Bonaparte with family-style meals. I think we should try it," suggested Amy.

Pete sighed, but he knew he should follow his wife's suggestion. He was hungry after his long walk. They'd stop and eat. Good thing school was out.

The next morning, Ron and Pete met with the great Ruby. She had volumes of material on Airliner Corks.

She began, "The company was started by Bernard Latcher. He is a chemical engineer who discovered a way to bind cork particles together by using a non-toxic resin. This was timed well, as Portugal experienced a cork tree disease, causing a shortage of cork for the wine industry. This also played into the hands of Congressman Joel Hanover. He, in one of his speeches, promised new job opportunities for his district. He immediately pushed the FDA to approve the manufacturing of recycled corks. It took two years, but he got his wish just before he was up for re-election.

"The very next January, he attached an amendment to the budget bill to grant Mr. Latcher funds to build and maintain his company for four years. He also specified that all restaurants within the government buildings within Washington be required to use only wine capped with Airliner recycled corks. Five years ago, Mr. Latcher launched his company here in Riverton. He employed 70 workers, which was a boon for Warren County. Restaurants, bars, inns, wineries, and anyone else who served wine collected their corks and shipped them to Riverton. There they were ground into a powder and mixed with the resin and re-formed into new bottle corks. His business expanded.

"Three years ago, the business started to falter. The internet doesn't explain, but soon Mr. Latcher built another facility on the other side of town. Little is known about this business except it is a subsidiary of Airliner Cork. The only product coming out of this company is small truckloads of ground cork. That's all I could find out."

"Great report. I should think we have enough information to pay Mr. Latcher a visit," said Pete. "On my walk around, I saw the plant is well kept. It might be a good investment."

"Now listen, Pete, we are on a contract with the SBA and not White and Lester Investment. We have to play this by the book," warned Ron.

"I suppose you are right, but it gives us a better perspective. I think we call Mr. Latcher and set up an appointment."

"What if he refuses?" asked the down-to-earth Ruby.

"Then we get real aggressive and offer him a buyout he can't refuse. It's four o'clock, I'll call him tomorrow, Rube."

Tuesday morning, Pete placed a call to Airliner Cork.

"Airliner Cork, may I help you?" said the voice at the other end.

"This is Pete White of Lester and White. We are interested in investing in Airliner Cork. Could I speak to the owner?"

"Mr. Latcher will be out of the office until Wednesday, but I can have him call you when he returns. What is the number where I can reach you?"

"My number is 515-778-2233. Ask him to speak with Pete or Ron."

Now the wait would be three days, at least. Pete figured Mr. Latcher's first day back on the job would be too busy to visit. If he did not return the call by Friday, he would try again. Pete patiently waited on Friday. He gave Latcher until three o'clock. The phone rang at ten. It was Mr. Latcher.

"Pete White."

"Mr. White, this is Bert Latcher. My assistant, Carol, told me you called. You indicated you and your partner might be interested in investing in Airliner Cork."

"Yes, sir, that is right. Ron and I are always interested in small firms to help grow or buy outright."

"Right now, neither Airliner nor Riverton Recycling are for sale. I investigated your firm and see you buy and sell in troubled companies, reallocate their assets, and resell them at a profit. Well, my company is not in trouble financially, and seventy families depend on the plant. If I let you buy in or purchase outright, these employees would probably lose their jobs. I'm afraid I cannot let that happen."

"I understand, Mr. Latcher. We are not trying to upset the apple cart, and we know the value of jobs in your county. Until we know more about Airliner Cork and Riverton Recycling, we cannot promise job security. I will assure we would do our best to maintain its viability."

"I'm sure you might, but it still isn't for sale. I found another website for a consulting firm called R&P Consulting. The owners were listed as Peter White and Ronald Lester. Is this the same two men who own the Lester & White Firm?"

"Yes, it is," answered Pete. He was surprised by the inquiry, but on the other hand, he could see an inroad to Airliner Cork.

Pete continued, "We have actually dropped most of the Lester & White business and have concentrated on the consulting business. It took less travel time, and both Ron and I are home with our families more. We would be glad to talk to you about your business and suggest changes if necessary. Our policy is the first visit is on our clock, and if you feel we cannot do you any good, it costs you nothing."

"I like the sound of that. I'd be free next week, either Tuesday or Wednesday. Would either date work out for you?"

"Just a second . . . Ruby, how's our calendar for next Tuesday or Wednesday? Wednesday is best . . . What time will suit you, Mr. Latcher?"

"How about ten in the morning? If we go longer, we can have lunch at the café."

"Sounds great! See you next Wednesday at ten o'clock."

Ron and Pete spent the next four days studying and analyzing Airliner Cork. They wanted to know everything possible about the company. Wednesday morning, they left Muscatine at eight. They calculated the trip would take just short of two hours. If they arrived early, they would tour the town.

They arrived in Riverton at 9:45, with fifteen minutes to kill. They drove to the town park on the Des Moines River. Ron checked back with Ruby, and Pete studied his questions. He was hopeful he would not make a mistake and reveal the real purpose of their visit. At 9:55, they headed for the factory and arrived precisely at 10:00.

The receptionist met them at the door. She was a small, petite lady with the reddest hair Pete had ever seen. Her face and arms were covered with hundreds of freckles. He couldn't help but wonder if her whole body was decked out that way. She wore a crisp white blouse, blue jeans, and tennis shoes. Evidently, casual was the dress code in this office.

"I'm Carol. I trust you two are the gentlemen from Lester & White, or should I say, R & P Consultants?" she asked them.

"R & P Consultants," returned Pete with a smile on his face.

This lady evidently was clued in on the same name, same company scheme. Looking beyond her, Ron spotted only one other woman in the office.

"Bert is expecting you. Come right on in. Sherry, will you buzz Bert for us?"

In less than two minutes, a tall man with hair graying at his temples appeared. He was nothing like Pete expected. With a name like Bertrand, he had pictured a nerd with big glasses and sweater. This guy could pose for a fashion magazine. The man quickly traversed the small office and stuck out his hand.

"Bert Latcher," he said. "And you are?"

"Pete White."

"Ron Lester."

"Pleased to meet you. Let's go into my office. Carol, would you bring in some coffee?"

They entered Bert's office. It wasn't very big, just enough room for one desk and three chairs. One wall was lined with file cabinets. On top of them were piles of folders and papers. Ron could tell Bert was an engineer and not a bookkeeper. He had to clear a spot to sit for himself. Carol arrived with the coffee and a box of doughnuts from the local Stop and Shop.

"Okay, gentlemen, where do we start?"

Pete looked at Ron, then said, "First, we'd like to tour the plant, or plants, as the case might be."

"Sure thing, but first let me tell how I got into this business. I'm a chemical engineer by trade. I got this idea about recycling corks in college. It took me a while, but after several years of smelling up our house and basement, I formulated a resin which I thought was non-toxic, odor free, and relatively inexpensive. I work with all kinds of plans and ideas. Finally, I discovered by grinding the used cork into a fine powder, it could be poured into molds and become new corks."

"Now I had the idea, but no money. Enter my friend and now Congressman, Joel Hanover. He promised new jobs for our district, which is rated near the poverty level by federal standards. With his help, I received a loan from the Small Business Administration. I bought this building from the local co-op. It had been a corn storage unit for them. It wasn't long and I had me a viable business employing 70 people, 45 here in this plant and 25 over at RRI. That's how I got started. The real story lies in how I have maintained production since then, but first let's tour the plant."

Bert led them out into the plant. Everyone was working. The dock was busy. Shipping was busy. They stopped at the first machine. It had four women and one man manning the operation.

Bert described the purpose of the station. "This machine is what I call the de-tailer. We found out that wine penetrates into each cork to about 30% of the depth of the cork. These ladies sort out the broken and damaged corks.

Sam here rakes the good corks into the machine, which slices off the bottom third of each cork. The top two thirds advance to a hammer mill grinder. The bottom third is fed into a roller mill and is bagged for delivery to a cattle-feeding yard ten miles north of town. We discovered the bottom third contains some sugars and carbohydrates. It can be mixed with silage and fed to cattle. All these byproducts are handled by Riverton Re-Cycling."

The trio continued through the plant. Next was the grinding room. Here Bert explained how the remaining cork material was ground to a powder and sent to the mixer next door. The mixer introduced the resin, which was thoroughly mixed with the cork particles to form a paste. From there, the paste was sent to the setting room, where different sets of trays were filled. There were as many trays as there were different shapes of corks. Some were specific to an individual winery. Finally, at the end of the line, all corks were inspected and packed into shipping boxes for shipping.

"That's about it," said Bert with a grin.

Pete asked, "Where does the recycling company come in?"

Bert gave him a wary eye and replied, "I told you, they take care of the cork refuse and package it for feed."

Pete continued to question him. "According to your website, Riverton Recycling has 25 employees. Certainly they do more than bag a bunch of cork particles."

Bert hesitated, then said, "Well, we do make some cork bricks for playgrounds with the imperfect stoppers. So far no one has complained about them."

"So there have been some problems with the corks?" inquired Ron.

Again Bert hesitated. "Yes, some."

He nervously looked around the busy production area.

"Why don't we go back to the office and I'll explain the situation."

"Sounds like a plan," Pete answered.

They walked back to the office without going through the Riverton Recycling building. Bert spun around in his chair. He shuffled through a pile of folders and threw them on the desk.

He opened by saying, "I wasn't going to let you guys in my plant, but the more I thought about it, I wondered if maybe your consulting firm could help me. I am the sole owner of this company. As Harry Truman said, the buck stops here. Everything I have accomplished is above the table and legal. I already know the SBA is becoming curious on how I operate. I have made all my payments on time. The only reason I can guess they are worried is because I have multiple grants from many government agencies. I think they think I am robbing Peter to pay Paul. In some ways, they are right. I do use money from one agency to pay others. I'm sure you already have discovered my congressman is responsible for my existence. This is the showcase of his district. He uses it for his political gain. I, on the other hand, used his influence to receive funds to run my company.

"At first, everything was great. Our product was accepted by many Midwest wineries. Our corks were cheaper and more durable. When we inserted the option of metal cork removers embedded in the resin corks, it added more markets. Within a year we went from thirty employees to one hundred twenty and three shifts. Our production rose to 500,000 corks per week, and we hadn't tapped into the California or New York markets. We were recycling wine cork from St. Louis, Chicago, Omaha, Milwaukee, and as far away as Minneapolis. There were several small firms emerging from those areas dealing exclusively in used cork collection and storage. This boom lasted for two years. We had 25% of the cork business in the U.S. I figured we would capture another 15% of the market. California was not on our radar. They seemed to rely on the conventional cork industry. They made false claims our cork with the resin contaminated the wine in the bottle. They ran our corks through many testing laboratories. This was costly and time consuming."

"They tried another angle. Some of the growers in Napa Valley had relatives owning and working the cork groves in Portugal. We were cutting in on their market. Next we knew, the Portuguese government threatened to boycott our exports of grain and meats into their country if the U.S. did not curtail our production. I received a letter from the USDA and the Department of Commerce stating we should cut our production by 50% or face a tax on our product. I started proceedings to sue the federal government for unjust taxation, but it is still tied up in the courts. In the meantime, they slapped an injunction on us to make us comply."

"Next, for some reason, the FDA labs discovered a trace amount of resin in one bottle of wine. It was three parts per billion. They claimed it might cause cancer if ingested in large amounts. The report didn't state what a large amount was. It came later, a large enough amount to cause cancer in rats would translate to consuming ten gallons of wine per day for six months.

"This report was followed by an inspection by OHSA. They found excess dust in our working place. We had to install extra air filters and air cleaners. I was just about to close the plant out of frustration, until of all people, an Amish lad suggested we try for some government grants. How he knew about these grants, I'll never know. He also explained there were people who write grants for a living. He said he couldn't do it because of his family. I took his advice and hired a professional grant writer.

"So the new way of life began. First, I received a grant, which means no payback, from the EPA for the ventilation fans and filters. Next, we went after the disposal of the corks and received another grant. The town needed some new housing, so we worked a grant from HUD to build new houses. We had to cut staff, but the Department of Labor gave us money to keep jobs here because we were in a poverty-stricken area. The jobs were necessary to keep the employees from the unemployment lines. The State of Iowa became involved in order to keep the unemployment rate low. They offered tax increment financing to help keep the plant open. Money flowed in from many places.

"To keep the recycled cork from the landfills, we received a grant to expand the recycling plant if we could find a place for the recycled material. The USDA granted us funds to test the corks for feed value in cattle. We were able to recycle 70% of our production. One weekend I called an employee meeting. Someone jokingly said, 'Why don't we make corks out of the re-cycled corks?'

"We all looked at each other. Although we all laughed, the idea was valid. All we had to do was find a way to wash the resin out of the corks which were just manufactured, load them in a truck, ride around town, and deliver the used cork to the receiving door of Airliner. Airliner re-manufactures the cork and sends them back to Riverton Recycling for processing. It became a vicious circle. We added cork material from some local recycler in Ottumwa, Des Moines, and Burlington. We've been doing the same for six years. We have provided jobs for seventy people, which means approximately 150 people are benefitting from this run-around. The problem is, we are running out of options and grants to tap. I'm afraid I will have to close the plant and all my employees will be affected, including me. They depend on this business for their livelihood. What do you suggest?"

Pete and Ron both couldn't believe what they had just heard. Here was a company which was seemingly put out of business because of world politics, but they managed through government programs and grants to continue to operate for six years. They were amazed.

Ron was the first to speak. "I think you should find another outlet for your cork-filled resin."

"What about floor tile or wall boards or bulletin boards? You have a resin which is non-toxic to humans. It must be non-toxic to pets, also. How about manufacturing a non-toxic cork tile for schools with kindergarten classes? Those tykes are on the floor all the time. I think veterinary clinics would be interested in such a product, too," added Pete.

He continued. "With all your experience in writing for grants, there has to be a start-up grant from some government agency. I'd apply again. If it would help, I think Lester & White would be interested in investing in Airliner Cork. What do you say, Ron?"

"I think there would be some challenges in the move, but it would get out from under the bottle cork injunction and any fight with the Portuguese government. I'm sure your Congressman would support your efforts. I also feel the State of Iowa would be happy to give tax breaks to anyone who creates jobs in the state," answered Ron.

Now Bert looked relieved and excited at the same time.

"I could contact Iowa State University and maybe they would have some students willing to help develop a new format. I could also save the jobs of my employees. I'm sure glad you fellows showed up."

Ron turned to Pete and said, "Pete, would you meet with me outside of a minute? I think there is something we should discuss before we go any further."

"Okay."

The two stepped outside. They made sure they were alone before Ron spoke.

"Pete, do you remember why we were originally sent here?"

"Yes, to investigate this company for the SBA and other government agencies."

"Are we doing that?"

"In a way."

"What do you plan to report to Miss Hot Stuff?"

We'll say she can report to the SBA, HUD, OSHA, NLB, FDA, USDA, REAP and the GOA that everything is aboveboard and legal."

"Hmmm. I guess everything is fine. The company is solvent and because of the help from the many federal agencies, Airliner Cork will continue to provide jobs for the area. We see a lesser need for government help as time goes by."

"What about Bert? He seems to be so concerned about his employees. Do we tell him the truth about why we are here?"

"I say yes. The truth is always best. Heck, if hadn't been for Miss Huseman, we'd never found out about Airliner Cork. I think if we explain everything to Bert and to Miss Huseman, everyone will understand the situation. Miss Huseman will look good to her bosses. Bert will look good to his employees and the community. We look good for not only reporting our findings, but we might be investing in a growing company. It will be a win, win, win situation all around."

"I agree. Let's go back and confess our dastardly deed to Bert, take him and Carol out to dinner, and head home to fill out our report for Miss Heather Huseman, government agent."

The pair returned inside and explained their purpose for being there. Bert at first was upset, but soon realized that if Pete and Ron hadn't appeared, he might being closing down his company. Now he could remain in this little Iowa town and provide employment for his neighbors. There might even be a chance to grow.

He called to Carol in the next office. "Carol, call down to The Factory Restaurant and make reservations for four. We are going out for lunch."

"Four?" she called back.

"Yes, four. You're going along, and I think when we get back, we're going to plan a company picnic."

"Okay."

Bert turned to Pete and Ron and said, "You and your families will attend, too. Won't they?"

"Yes. Most certainly," they answered in unison.

Two weeks later the picnic was held. All the town was invited. There were games and food and prizes. The only glitch in the ointment was when Heather Huseman arrived unannounced.

"Oh, oh, here comes trouble." stated Pete, "we'd better get over to Bert and run some interference."

Heather was dressed this day in a light blue business pant suit with a blue floral blouse underneath and matching blue pumps. She looked as if she could have stepped right out of a fashion magazine. She carried an envelope in her hand as she smartly walked across the grass. Tension was in the air as she headed for Bert.

'Mr. Latcher, I have received the report from R & P Consulting. I'm afraid your business practices are suspect. I'm going to order an audit of your operation. If they find you fraudulent, they will prosecute. I have a subpoena for you and your consultants."

Bert took the envelope and was about to open it when Pete arrived.

"Is there anything I may help with?" he asked.

Miss Huseman explained the SBA's position and the consequences of an audit.

"Do you really think that would be necessary, Miss Huseman?" replied Ron, who had just arrived, "Pete and I sent you all the material we thought necessary."

"I must follow the rules, Mr. White. I don't make the decisions. They are made in Washington."

"But look at the people Mr. Latcher has helped. Many in this community would be on welfare if they didn't have this company. I think you should reconsider. You realize this whole project was started by Congressman Joel Hanover. He may see it differently."

"I'm well aware of the Congressman's interest in this area. He will receive a full report."

"But Miss Huseman, many families depend on this company; otherwise, they would be on welfare or be forced to leave Riverton. This company is vital to the economy of this region. The fact that it runs entirely on loans and grants is the fault of the government not Mr. Latcher. I feel you should reconsider your accusations and look at the human factors presented here. This man has given many hours to help this town and without him and his company it would not exist."

Pete butted in, "I must also add, Miss Huseman, Mr. Latcher is developing new products as we speak. He is trying to use the cork material in a more efficient manner. The first product off his production line will be floats for under swimming pool covers. Cork is much better than plastic and is organic."

Miss Huseman paused, "I will take your information to my superiors and get back with you. You do have a valid case, but again I will need more information about these new products since they have been introduced after this report.. You should know in a couple of months."

"Would you care to join us, Miss Huseman?" asked Bert trying to change the subject.

She smiled at Bert and said, "I'd liked to but that might be considered a bribe, so I'll have to decline. Rules are rules."

"I understand."

With that being said she turned and smartly walked away.

All three men watched as she returned to her car.

Bert turned to Pete and said, "Pete, I don't have any cork floats being manufactured. I don't even have a R & D department."

"I know that, but she doesn't and the government doesn't. By the time they re-process you'll have to have those floats and a R&D staff. At least, she is not going to spoil our picnic."

Heather back her car out of its parking spot and turned toward Main Street. She rolled down her window and gave the men a wave.

"Now, that young lady is a piece of class." said Ron.

"Yes, and she works for the government. I never would have guessed a good looking dame like her would work for SBA especially in Iowa. She more suited for Chicago." added Pete with a chuckle.

All three had a good laugh as they walked back to the picnic area.

What If

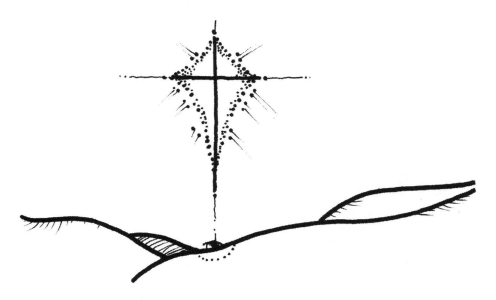

Most residents of the world believe in a higher being or power. There are the three major religions of Christianity, Judaism, and Islam. They all believe in the one God. Obviously, they all take different views of the deity.

Even the Native Americans believed in something or someone being a higher power. The Greeks, the Italians, the Scandinavians all had their different gods to explain the unexplainable. In the Far East there are the Buddhists, Hindus, and many other religions. All religions exist to help us explain the unknown.

So if you are a believer in God, the Father, you have heard the story of the Garden of Eden and the couple who lived there. We have those who believe the Bible literally and those who don't. Any way you look at it, man has only been in existence for a short time. His weak theories have been discussed and argued for centuries. The earth has existed for millions of years. This higher being or beings we all believe in, called gods, are a patient bunch. Since I believe in one God, I am going to concentrate on His actions. Since I also proclaim to be loyal to the Christian faith, I also believe in the existence of His Son, Jesus.

Time means little to God, it seems. We have had many wars and conflicts dating back ten thousand years. If you read the Bible, you will soon find out how the so-called people of God's own choosing wavered to and from His care. Their history only goes back a few thousand years. We know from uncovering dinosaurs and other ancient creatures that the earth has been around for millions of years. So what is a thousand years or more to God when He has existed for millions of years?

This is where my story starts. What if God decided to wait to send His Son, Jesus, until our year 2000? If this is the case, then everyone up to that date would either be Jewish, Muslim, a Far East religion, or some other pagan religion, for there would be no Christianity.

In this scenario, I let the Jewish people discover the Americas. They were being persecuted in Asia and Europe by non-Judean faiths. America promised freedom for God's chosen people. They migrated by the thousands. They established a democratic government with their capital, New Jerusalem, located in an independent District of Abraham. They became a powerful nation reminiscent of the Israel of King David.

The only drawback was the recent decay of the morals of people. Drinking and drugs are rampant. Unwed mothers continue to have multiple babies form multiple fathers. Couples live together without any commitment. Crime is out of control. Gangs and mobs rule the big cities. Politicians cheat and are easily bribed. The law is not respected. No one trusts anyone. The "good" people of the earth, God's people, are still waiting for their Messiah. How bad will it become before this king arrives?

Joe Feinstein lived in Nazareth, Indiana, and was a carpenter by trade. He started working for his father at the age of twelve. By eighteen, he was an experienced carpenter. His father insisted Joe go to college. When his father suffered a heart attack and died during his freshman year, Joe returned home to finish the homes his father had started. He never returned to college. His small company of two employees custom built houses and other small buildings. He was handsome, young, and strong from his years of outside work. He had dark curly hair and a chiseled face. His smile was infectious and all the young women adored him.

Mary Kruger lived on the poor side of town. She was a beautiful young woman, not cute but regal. Her dark brown hair framed her Grecian face. Her deep brown eyes glistened with kindness. She was of average height at about five foot six. Her father was an alcoholic and her mother worked as a housekeeper. Mary attended high school where her friends thought her to be very shy and quiet. Although she was a good student, she never had a chance to further her education.

One of her many jobs was working at the local pizza parlor. One evening she served pizza to Joe. He was infatuated with her beauty and her sweet voice. Soon he was walking her home after work. Within a year, he asked Mary to be his wife. She readily accepted. Her father was elated, for he would get rid of the liability of raising his daughter. Her mother was glad just to have her daughter married and away from home.

The wedding was not planned until spring of the next year. April seemed like a good month. Joe would not be busy yet and the weather for an outdoor wedding would be possible. The local synagogue had built a small wedding chapel behind the main building for such occasions. The rabbi was contacted to reserve the date. He recommended marriage counseling for the couple. He would schedule those meetings during the winter months when Joe's work was slower. Mary continued to work as a waitress. On her off days, Joe hired her to paint some interior rooms at his new home sites. They both counted the days until their nuptial.

One warm evening in late July, Joe received a phone call from Mary. He could tell she was upset over something. He hurried to Mary's home. When he arrived, he found Mary seated next to the kitchen table. She was wearing an oversized T-shirt and baggy shorts. Her hair was a mess. Her eyes were red from crying. Her mother, Anne, was standing by the stove in her old cotton robe and terry cloth slippers. Joe had seldom seen Anne wear anything else. She had a concerned look on her face.

Joe said quickly, "What happened? Did someone die?"

Anne answered before Mary had a chance, "No, nothing like that. It is something which happened to Mary. Now Joe, my Mary is a wonderful girl. She'd do nothing to hurt you. You must believe her and trust her. She's pre--"

Mary interrupted, "Mom, I'll take it from here. Why don't you go to the family room and watch some TV."

Anne glared at her daughter with disapproval, but she left the kitchen. She wanted to be part of the coming conversation.

By now, Joe was perplexed. What could be so terrible?

"All right, Mary, what's this all about?"

Mary pulled a chair from the table and turned it toward her. She said, "Please sit down, Joe. I have something to tell you."

"Okay."

"But I don't know where to start."

"How about the beginning?"

"Okay, about four months ago, I came home from work. It had been a long day because one of the girls became sick, so I had to do a shift and a half. When I got home, the house was dark. I found a note from my mother stating she had gone over to Aunt Elizabeth's to help her with house cleaning. You know my Aunt Elizabeth is expecting a baby, don't you?"

"Yes."

"I no more than got inside the door and the phone rang. It was Mom. Aunt Lizzy was in a great deal of pain, so she was staying over till morning. That was okay with me. I was so tired. I opened a can of soup for supper and made some cocoa. While the soup was heating, I changed into my pajamas and slippers. I turned on the TV and the ten o'clock news was on. I sat down the on couch and had my little meal. I watched a little Jay Leno and headed to bed. I was in the bathroom, brushing my teeth, when I remembered to lock the back door and check the front door. Everything was tightly locked. I returned to my bedroom and fell into bed. I was fast asleep when I heard this voice calling, 'Mary, Mary, wake up.'

"I opened one eye and there at the edge of my bed was a figure. It looked like a man, only he was brilliantly dressed in white and glistened as the whitest snow. There was an aura of light surrounding him. On his back, I could see what I thought were wings. You can imagine how I jumped. I screamed, 'Who are you?'

"He answered, 'I am Gabriel, a messenger from God. Do not be afraid for I bring you good news, Mary, for the Almighty God has chosen you. You will bear His Son and he will save the world. As it is written in Isaiah, A virgin will bear a son and He will be call Emmanuel, Prince of Peace. You, my fair lady, are that virgin.'"

Joe butted in. "Do you expect me to believe that an angel of God actually appeared to you?"

"Y-y-yes! I'm not telling you a lie," Mary cried, her voice quivering. "I didn't think it was possible either, but there he was. At first I was frightened, but his calming voice and smile convinced me he meant no harm. He disappeared as mysteriously as he appeared. I didn't tell anyone because I was sure no one would believe me. I didn't even tell Mom until . . . "

"Until what?" quizzed Joe.

"Until I started to feel something in my stomach area. There was this twinge. I told my Mom about the feeling. Her first reaction was, I was pregnant. I told her

I couldn't be. I never slept with anyone. Then I remembered the angel telling me God would make me pregnant and I was to bear His son. Now I have missed several periods and I feel something growing inside me. Joe, I'm not lying. You've got to believe me. I wouldn't cheat on you. I promised I wouldn't."

Joe sat quietly and stared at his fiancée. He didn't know what to say. He loved Mary. How could she do this to him? He rose from his chair and said, "I want to believe you, but I just can't right now. I'm leaving, Mary. Don't try to stop me. I just have to have some time to figure this out."

He turned and walked out the door. Mary ran after him, crying. She called out as he got into his pickup, "Papa will kick me out when he finds out. Please believe me."

Joe slammed his door and stomped on the gas. The tires squealed as he pulled away. Mary returned to the house and into the waiting arms of her mother.

"Mama, what am I going to do? You know Papa. He'll be furious."

"Right now we will send you to Elizabeth's and not tell him. If what you say is true, and I believe it is, God will protect you. After all, you, my dear daughter, are going to bear God's child."

Joe was fuming. How could this happen? He decided to take a drive through the park on his way home. In fact, he might even take a walk. Maybe then, when he was alone, he could sort out his feelings and his next step. He pulled the truck into the little parking lot at the trail head. There were no other vehicles in the lot. He started down the isolated trail.

He had gone about a block when he found a bench along the trail. He sat and closed his eyes. As he sat there, he heard a rustling in the leaves. He opened his eyes and there right beside him was a man. The man was dressed in white from head to toe. He was so white he glistened in the fading light. Where did he come from? There was no one else on the pathway. The park seemed empty.

"Joseph Ruben Feinstein?" the man asked.

"Yes, how do you know my name?"

"Oh, I know many things about you, Joe. You are a carpenter. You own our own company. You are in love with a beautiful woman named Mary Rachel Krueger."

"Well, you're right on the first two statements. But in love with Mary, I doubt it anymore."

"Joe, I know you just left Mary when she told you she was pregnant."

"Yes, I did, but how do you know all these things? Are you an angel or something?"

"I thought you'd never ask. Yes, I am Gabriel, a messenger from God Almighty. I am the one who talked to your fiancée, Mary. She is telling the truth, Joe. She carries the son of God. She has not been with anyone. She is still a virgin by human standards. When she delivers this son, you are to name him Jesus. He will be the Messiah, the Savior of the earth. Go back to her and ask for forgiveness. She needs you. God, my boss, will protect you and Mary."

"I hear what you are saying, but how do I know if you are really an angel?"

"Let me see. Joe, do you see that tree over there by the stream?"

"Yes."

"Watch it."

The tree was a gnarled, twisted, half-dead box elder hanging over the water. Gabriel reached out with his hand and pointed toward the broken tree. It immediately straightened and stood tall. The dead branches fell off and new leaves appeared.

"Wow! That was impressive. I guess you are an angel," said Joe. When he turned to say something else, Gabriel had disappeared. Joe muttered to himself and started back toward the parking lot. He took one more look at the twisted tree and found it was back to its original shape.

I must be dreaming, he thought. *Who would believe I saw an angel? Well, maybe Mary.*

As he approached the lot he could see his pickup was tilted a bit. He hurried to the opposite side and sure enough, there was a flat tire on the truck. He grumbled some more. "What else could go wrong?"

He knelt down by the tire as most people do just to check if it really flat. As he did, he felt a tap on his shoulder. He turned and looked up. There was Gabriel again.

"You aren't convinced yet, are you, Joe?"

Joe was so dumbfounded, he couldn't speak.

"I suppose you can fix this tire," he said sarcastically.

Gabriel didn't answer, but he did bend down and with his hand he extracted a silver nail from the tread. He handed it to Joe and said, "Keep this as a reminder of our visit."

Next he spit on his fingers and touched the hole in the tire. He blew toward the flattened tire and it filled with air.

"Now do you believe in me?"

"Yes!"

"Do you love Mary?"

"Yes!"

"Then go to her and tell her so. Ask her to marry you right now. Forget the big wedding ceremony next year. I will send a rabbi to do the ceremony tonight. Hurry before her father comes home. Trust God to help you. It is His Son she carries and He will protect you. Now go."

Gabriel turned to go, then stopped and continued, "Oh, by the way, I'll be back to see you when Mary delivers the child."

Joe hopped into the pickup and returned to Mary's home. Along the way he pondered what the angel said. The angel seemed so real. It had to be true.

Joe slid to a stop in front of Mary's house. He ran up the sidewalk and knocked on the door. Mary answered the door, surprised to see him.

"Oh, Joe, you came back. I thought I'd never see you again. Come on in."

"Mary, let's get married. I had this angel tell me to believe you. He said God would protect us, then he performed a couple of miracles to convince me. Let's not wait. We have to be done before your father gets home."

"But where can we find a rabbi at this late hour?"

"The angel said he would take care of it."

"Mary, come help me with your bags," called her mother from upstairs.

"Coming, mother," she answered.

Mary and Joe both entered the stairway.

"Here, let me help," said Joe.

Anne was completely surprised to see Joe. She dropped the two heavy pieces of luggage with a thud.

"Joe, you came back. By the blessing of the Lord God, I never thought I'd see you again. Why did you come back?"

"It's a long story, Mrs. Kruger, but let's just say an angel told me to return and marry your daughter immediately."

Anne clamored down the steps as fast as she could and hugged and kissed Joe.

"Joe, I'm so happy. Mary will make you a good wife. And Joe, call me Anne or Mom, not Mrs. Krueger. We're going to be family now, right?"

"Right," Joe said with a smile.

He went up the steps and carried down Mary's luggage. Just as he finished, there was a knock on the front door. Mary's mother answered it. It was Rabbi James and his wife, Martha.

The rabbi spoke first. "I was told there is a couple who need to be married living here."

Joe stuck his head around the kitchen door. "That's right, Rabbi. Mary and I would like your services, but how did you know to come now?"

The rabbi smiled. "I was putting the Torah away from our services when this man dressed in white appeared."

"Was his name Gabriel?"

"Why, yes, it was. How did you know that?"

"Just a guess because he appeared to me a little earlier and said he would contact a rabbi."

Mary entered the room and heard the conversation. She added, "He appeared to me several months ago."

"Well, well, well, I guess we have something important going on. Our Creator must be working on something big. I think we should honor His wishes. We should get on with the ceremony. Do we have any wine glasses?"

"We sure do," answered Anne. "They are not expensive ones, but they will do."

"Good, then let's proceed," answered Rabbi James, "I was wondering why I found this marriage certificate on my desk just about an hour ago. I guess the Almighty had a hand in that, too."

The ceremony was short. Joe kissed Mary and the new couple exited in Joe's pickup. They weren't going far, just to Joe's place. The honeymoon would happen later. Of course, Mary's father was furious and he forbade Mary from ever coming home again. She did, however, sneak in when her father was working or spending time at the local pub.

The months flew by. In November, there was a national election. The new administration was concerned about who was Jewish and who was not. There was a public outcry, but he got his way. By his decree everyone in America was to be counted in a special census. Since the Jewish faith still put much emphasis on the patriarchal side of the family, Joe would have to go to his father's home town of Bethlehem to fill out the forms. The government did not trust the internet or mail-in forms. They thought there was too much chance of fraud.

The census was to take place the first two weeks after Hanukah. The only problem was, Mary was to deliver at the same time. Could she stand the ride to Bethlehem?

On the very first day of the census, Joe loaded the very pregnant Mary into his truck. They headed for the one-hundred-mile trek to the town of his roots. The weather channel predicted a major snow and ice storm was on its way. Joe wanted to beat the oncoming weather.

He reached the office of the census bureau, but there was a long line already ahead of him. He waited impatiently. The line moved slowly. Mary waited in the pickup, only getting out to journey to the ladies' restroom. She felt a little discomfort, but being her first pregnancy she thought it was pain from the long ride there.

It was almost four when Joe returned. The storm had caught them. The wind and rain started first, followed by freezing rain with snow, as predicted. The roads north of town were being closed by the highway patrol. The motel and hotels filled quickly. Joe was reluctant to stay, but by the time they were ready to hit the interstate, the highway patrol closed the road south also. Joe turned around and tried to find a place to stay. His gas gauge was reading low. He pulled into a service station. The station was old style, but it was on the right side of the street. He filled the tank and went inside to speak to the owner.

"Do you know of any other motels in Bethlehem? I called three and they are all full. My wife needs to take a rest before we journey on."

"Sorry," was the answer. "Have you tried the B&B down the street?"

"Yes, and they have people sleeping in the lounge area. This storm is really causing a problem."

Joe was going to buy some candy bars and looked outside to see Mary trudging to the restroom.

The owner said, "Is that your wife?"

Joe smiled and replied, "Yes, we're expecting a baby any time. We had to come for this darn census. She really needs a rest now. I guess we will try our best in the truck."

The owner thought a minute. "Say, I could let you stay in the back room of the station. I've got a cot there. I used to sleep there when we were open 24 hours. When they opened the Quikstop across the street, it really slowed down my business, so I don't use it anymore. There's blankets and an oil-burning stove for heat. It would come in handy if the power goes off. You and your wife are welcome to have it. I'm about ready to close. Drive around back and I'll meet you there."

"Oh, thank you, thank you, sir. Right now anything is appreciated."

With Mary back in the truck, Joe pulled into the alley behind the station. He helped Mary inside.

"It isn't much of a bed, ma'am, but it will be better than your truck. The heater is working. There are extra blankets on the shelf above the water heater. I'm sorry I can't do better."

"This will be fine, Mr.--?" said Mary.

"Mr. George."

"This will be fine, Mr. George. Thank you very much."

"Joe—that is your name, isn't it?"

"Yes."

"Joe, I must be going before the weather gets worse. I live about half a mile away and the missus will be worried."

"Thank you again, Mr. George. Now you hurry home. We'll be fine."

Mr. George went to the front of the station and turned off the outside lights. Just before he locked the front door he hollered out, "They have real good sandwiches across the street, if you are hungry."

Joe thanked him again and turned to Mary, who was trying to get some of the blankets.

"I'll sleep on the floor. You take the cot."

Mary wasn't arguing. She sat on the cot and lay on her side. Joe covered her.

"Now you sleep some, and we'll make it home tomorrow."

Mary sighed and spoke. "You know, Joe, I'm having these funny pains in my stomach. Do you suppose they may be labor pains?"

"Gosh, Mary, I hope not. Where would we go to the hospital? The nearest one is in Joppa, ten miles away. The roads are closed. Maybe they are just pains from riding so long."

"Maybe, Joe. I certainly hope so."

Mary lay on her side and tried to sleep. Joe laid on the floor next to the cot. Soon he was snoring. He was exhausted. Mary started to time the pains. They were getting closer and closer. At nine she shook Joe.

"Wake up, Joe. I need to go the hospital. The pains are ten minutes apart."

Just as she said that, the lights flickered and went out. Only the glow from the heater's firebox lit the tiny room. Joe woke with a jerk. He looked outside. The street, poles, tree limbs, and truck were covered with ice. He panicked. His only recourse was to call for help. He dialed 911.

"Emergency, how may I help you?" was the voice at the other end.

"This is Joe Feinstein. I'm at an old gas station on Grand Avenue across from the Quikstop. My wife is having a baby. I need help or an ambulance soon."

"I've got you located, sir, but I'm afraid I have some bad news. There has been a very bad accident on Interstate 63. All the ambulances are there. It will be an hour before we can get there and maybe more with all this ice."

Now Joe was really panicking. Mary was moaning more and more. She couldn't wait long. In fact, she was getting ready herself. She was stripping off her sweat pants.

"What am I to do?" Joe asked the lady at the other end.

"Where did you tell me you were located?"

"At the service station on Grand, across from the Quikstop."

"Are there any rags or towels around?"

"I don't know. I can check the other rooms, but first I have to find a flashlight. The lights went out about ten minutes ago."

"You look around, I'll stay on the line. If I leave you just holler, Katy! and I'll be back."

Joe fumbled his way into the front office. He looked under the counter and found a flashlight. He scrounged around in the shop area. He discovered some clean shop rags plus a stack of old towels, pieces of flannel shirts, two big rolls of paper towels, and a sheet of plastic. He gathered all he could in his arms and returned to the back room. He found Mary sitting on the cot. She was holding her swollen stomach.

"We can't wait much longer, Joe. The baby is coming."

"Just one more minute, honey."

Joe discovered an old wooden Pepsi bottle carrier. He broke out the dividers and lined it with the paper towels first, then the soft old flannel shirts.

"This will be our son's new cradle. God told us He would help us. I feel He is helping now. Now you lay back and remember what we were taught in the Lamaze classes. You start breathing and I'll watch the birthing process. We watched a birth on a screen, but we never thought we would being doing it ourselves. Let's do our best, Mary. You have to do all the work. I'll just assist. Now I have to get some warm water. I'll be right back."

He headed for the grease rack room. He found a dish pan on the back wall. He shone the flashlight in it. It looked clean. He filled it with warm water and returned to Mary. She had taken care of herself. She had laid the plastic sheet on the bed and covered it with a sheet. She was standing naked to her waist and a pool of liquid was spreading on the floor.

"My water broke and now you have a mess to clean up. I'm sorry."

"Don't worry, baby, it's the natural thing to happen. It is just amniotic fluid. It means it won't be long now."

A voice startled Joe.

"Joe, Joe, this is Katy from emergency. How are you doing?"

"I'm doing fine. It is Mary who has to do all the work. She is pushing and puffing. Tell me, when is the ambulance getting here?"

"I'm sorry to tell this you this, but our only ambulance in Bethlehem is in the ditch. It will be several hours before they will be there."

"With God's help we'll get through this. Just send the ambulance as soon as you can."

Joe gave the operator his phone number. She said would call back in ten minutes. By now, Mary was pushing hard. Joe tried to remember the scenes in the Lamaze class.

They worked together and the birthing went well. Mary delivered her baby boy. Joe bathed the child and dried him with some of the old rags he had found. He wrapped him in a piece of flannel and laid him in the Pepsi bottle case. He returned to Mary and helped her bathe. She laid back, exhausted.

"Take a short nap, honey. When you wake up, you can nurse our new boy."

"You better call Katy back and tell her everything is fine. Oh, and tell her we named him Jesus."

Joe didn't have to make the call. Katy was ahead of him.

"How are you two doing?" she asked.

"Fine. Mary is napping. The baby is also sleeping. He is so healthy."

"Great! They have the ambulance on the road again. They have to return to the accident scene on I-63 one more time, then they will come to check on you. By the way, have you named him yet?"

"Oh, yes. God told us to name him Jesus."

"Jesus. That is a different name. It is one I've never heard before, but I like it. Well, best of luck to you and your wife, Joe. I'm going off shift in ten minutes. Ruth Ann will be here to answer the calls. She will inform you when the ambulance crew will arrive."

Joe said, "Okay, we'll be waiting."

About ten miles south of Bethlehem, two brothers had two farms bordering each other. Eli and his wife, Naomi, raised purebred Dorset sheep. They owned fifty ewes plus six rams. His brother, Levi, and his wife, Martha, were commercial sheep herders. Their flock was much larger at 250 ewes. They raised their sheep for wool production and lambs. The two shepherds worked together. Eli's sheep flock was a second job. He worked as a fertilizer salesman for the local co-op. Levi was the farmer-shepherd. Along with his larger flock, he farmed 400 acres of crop ground.

Tonight both men were watching the storm. At nine o'clock in the evening, the storm subsided. Levi told Martha he was going to check the flock before the ten o'clock news. He wanted to make sure all his ewes were safe and inside. He was planning to have them sheared in two weeks, and this time of the year, keeping the wool dry was always a struggle. He headed for the barn. He looked over at Eli's barn. The lights were on, and Eli was also checking his flock. He walked through the back lot and saw Eli's flashlight.

"Hey, Eli, how are doing?"

"Fine, I'm just making sure I don't have any stragglers outside."

"Me, too."

Eli cocked his head and asked Levi, "Do you hear music?"

Levi paused and shook his head. "Yes. Where do you suppose it is coming from?"

They looked around and both men spotted a light which appeared to be hanging in the air.

"Is that a helicopter?" asked Levi.

"Could be, but I don't hear any noise that sounds like a copter. Let's walk toward it and see if we can find out what it is."

"It looks like it is near the crossover."

The two men started walking toward the light, each on their own side of the fence. They approached the crossover, a series of steps crossing over the fence, which protected the fence wire from damage by persons climbing over the fence. It also made it easier to pass from one side to the other. The light became brighter. All of a sudden, the music became louder. It was like a choir singing. Even though it was night, a light broke through the heavens. It became blinding bright. A figure floated down from the sky. Levi looked at Eli.

"They're coming to get us. We're going to die."

Eli jumped over the crossover and hugged Levi. They both knelt on the ground. The figure floated to the crossover and sat on the top step.

"W-w-w-who are you?" stammered Levi. He was so afraid his knees were shaking.

The figure appeared to be a man dressed in snow-white clothes that glowed. He raised his hand and said, "Be not afraid. I am Gabriel, a messenger from Almighty God, the Father. I have good news for you. Tonight, in Bethlehem, a babe was born. He will be the Savior of the world, The Prince of Peace, Emmanuel. God the Father wants you to go and witness the miracle birth."

"How will we find this baby?"

"Just look for the star. You will find the babe and his parents in the back room of an old Texaco service station on Grand Avenue. Go to the alley and you will find the door open. Despite the lack of electricity, they are warm. I will go ahead and inform them you are on the way. Now rise up and get your wives and go to Bethlehem. Hurry! Oh, another instruction, drive on the graveled back roads. The main highways are too icy."

With that, the heavens opened and thousands of angels appeared and began singing. The music was thunderous and beautiful. Levi and Eli stood in awe. They couldn't believe their eyes and ears.

Next they heard Gabriel calling them, "Get going! Hurry!"

The two men turned and trotted as fast as they could. At their age, running was out of the question. They stopped at Levi's barn.

Levi said, "You go and get Naomi. I'll get my Martha. We'll take my four-wheel drive pickup."

"Ten-four, brother. See you in ten minutes."

Ten minutes later, Levi and Martha arrived at Eli's. He was by himself.

"Isn't Naomi going?"

"Nah, I couldn't convince her. She wants to stay home and watch Jay Leno on the TV. She thinks I'm nuts anyway. Whoever talks to angels must be daft, she says. So let's go and do God's work and find this heavenly baby."

Eli piled into the back seat behind Martha. Levi shifted into four-wheel drive and off they drove. When they reached Grand Avenue at the edge of town, Levi said, "Now what? Which way do we go?"

"The angel said look for the star."

"There's no star out on a night like this."

Martha blurted out, "There's one, by that old service station. See it glowing a bright red?"

Sure enough, about two blocks away was a bright red star on a sign, illuminating the darkened street. The only lights were the few candles in the windows of the houses along the street. Levi turned down Grand Avenue. He turned right just before the station, since Gabriel had told him to enter the alley behind the station. There through the small back window glowed a flickering light.

"This must be the place," exclaimed Levi. "I'll check the door."

Levi got out and knocked on the door. He heard some shuffling inside and a voice calling, "Come in."

Levi motioned Eli and Martha to follow him. They crowded inside.

"Please come in and see our baby. The angel Gabriel told us you would be here. This is the Son of God. He is our Savior, our Prince of Peace, and Ruler of all nations. He is to be named Jesus, Emmanuel, Son of the living God."

The trio didn't know what to do at first. Then Martha knelt and worshipped the child lying in the wooden Pepsi crate. The two brothers followed her lead. Joe watched. Mary smiled as she patted her precious child. Time seemed to drag until another knock came at the door.

"Come in," said Joe.

Mr. George entered. His face showed surprise.

"May I ask who these people are?" he said, pointing at the trio.

"These are shepherds form south of town. They are here to worship our son."

"How did they find this place?"

Eli answered, "We saw the star on the sign."

"The sign. That sign hasn't been lit for years. You must be seeing things."

"No, it is lit. Go see for yourself."

Mr. George stepped outside. He hurried back in and cried, "It is lit. It's a miracle. I don't believe it, but I saw it with my own eyes. Please accept my apologies for my poor accommodations. Please come to my house."

"That won't be necessary, Mr. George. The 911 operator told me the ambulance would be here in a few minutes. We are going the clinic for a checkup and then, I hope, home. Thank you anyway."

Right after Joe said that, there were red lights flashing outside. Two EMTs entered. They checked the baby and asked Mary how she felt. They told her they would like her to go to the hospital for a checkup. She agreed to go if Joe could follow them.

"Of course," was the answer.

The EMTs helped Mary and the baby into the ambulance. Levi and Eli helped Joe scape the ice from the windshield of Joe's pickup. In a few minutes, he left. The shepherds and the station owner chatted about the evening. They said their good-byes and headed home.

On the way home, Eli said, "After tonight, with seeing a real-life angel, then the miracle star on the sign, and the birth of a child in the rear of a gas station, I believe there is a God and He is with us. This really changes my thoughts on religion, especially our faith. I believe I'll become a rabbi of a new church. I have you two, maybe Naomi, and I think I can convince some of those fishermen on the river."

It was a joyous ride home.

Many miles away, near Tucson, Arizona, is an observatory on the top of Mount Kitt. An astronomer was scanning the dark skies. All of a sudden it seemed three or four stars aligned themselves in a cluster. They were so closely bunched, to the naked eye, they looked like one bright star. He was astounded. Quickly he went to the computer to see if there was a formation recorded previously. There was none. The astronomer was overjoyed. He had discovered a new formation or galaxy or something. After taking photos and recording the finding, he hurried to his office and called his partner.

"Hello, Dr. Hiram Goldman here."

"Hiram, this is Rueben Sachs. I have made a phenomenal discovery. Four stars or maybe planets have aligned themselves to form one bright object in the sky. I'm asking you to come and verify this phenomenon. I have the computer taking photos as we speak. Hurry over before it disappears."

Hiram hurried to the observatory as quickly as possible. Luckily, he was working in the lab three blocks away. He viewed the star or stars. He backed up and blinked his eyes.

"I'm going to check every book and setting I know of. This is special."

The two men spent the next several hours examining data, charts, and histories. They found nothing.

"Let's sleep on it," suggested Rueben. "Maybe in the morning, something will reveal itself."

"Good idea, but I bet neither of us will sleep much," Hiram replied with a chuckle.

They each retired to their two-room apartment on the observatory complex. They would not go home to Tucson tonight. Hiram was right. Neither Reuben nor he slept very much. It was a good thing they were not home.

Hiram's phone rang in his room. It was Reuben.

"Got an idea. Isn't there some reference to a star in some of the old histories of the Jewish people? I mean, way back, several millenniums ago. Back where some of those ancient prophets like Isiah, Malachi, and Ezekiel were telling we Jews to repent."

"Could be. I'll bet Rabbi John would have some knowledge on that subject. I'll call him. Let me see. He lives in New York. That's three hours ahead of us, so it is seven o'clock there. He'll be up."

Hiram called John.

"What's up, my old friend?" answered John.

"My partner discovered an unusual star. In all our research, we cannot find any information of this phenomenon occurring. He suggested there might be a reference to it in the old history books of the Jewish faith."

"Don't know. Some of those books go back 4000 years."

"I know! Maybe some old prophecy has come true. Maybe God is getting tired of us down here and wants to try something different."

"Could be. I'll get my staff on it right away."

Within an hour, Rabbi John returned the call.

"I think we found the answer. In the old, old book of Numbers 24:17, it states a star will signal the coming of a new age. This new age will be led by this child. I think we should find this child and check on some other facts. Is he from the lineage of David? Is there a direct line from Abraham? We could check his DNA. There are too many unanswered questions right now. I'll keep my crew checking and try to narrow down the place where the event is to have happened."

It was a long day for the pair of astronomers. They checked and re-checked their figures. They were anxious for night. At midnight, they opened the cover on the telescope. The bright star was gone. It had disappeared. The four planets or stars were still there, but they were not as bright as the night before. The men were shocked. What happened? The night before was truly a phenomenon. Something only to be explained by an act of God. Now the quest to find this child or family was of greatest importance.

It was two weeks before Rabbi John called with his research.

"The prophets say in many places, the child will be born in the city of David, which is Bethlehem. Now there a zillion Bethlehems in the world. The most important one is in Israel. I would start there, but I don't think we will find much there. It was destroyed in the last conflict with the Muslim radicals. I suggest we search out each Bethlehem and check hospital records and court records. A birth on this day has to be recorded somewhere."

Reuben replied, "We will need some funding. I'll apply for a grant from the university right away."

"Let's plan on meeting in thirty days in Chicago. I have some contacts with the university there. I'm sure they will be interested, also," added Hiram.

Thirty days flew by. The three met in a conference room at the University of Chicago. Several other scholars were invited. They all agreed to the importance of the sighting. Rabbi John suggested the church sponsor the search. He was sure the head rabbis would approve. The conference closed with different options. The best seemed to be having the Jewish faith fund the search.

Rabbi John quickly called the headquarters. He explained the event. The Chief Rabbi asked Rabbi John to come to Jerusalem and give them more information. Rabbi John, Hiram, and Reuben all journeyed to Jerusalem. They explained their findings. The top officials acted as if they were interested. They would fund the search.

"If and when you find this child, let us know so we can also worship him and become more informed of his importance."

The trio were elated. They started their search right away. With cameramen, recorders, secretaries, and their families, they went to every town named Bethlehem. They checked court records, hospital records, and interviewed residents. Three years later, they were down to their last Bethlehem. It was a very small town in Indiana.

They pulled into a Quikstop on Grand Avenue. Their entourage of trucks and personnel attracted attention. The crew went inside for some snacks. Reuben stayed outside with his wife, Miriam.

She said, "Isn't that a quaint gas station across the street. I bet they are closed."

Miriam spotted a man in the window, and being a very inquisitive person, she walked across the street.

"Sir," she asked the man, "you look like a man who knows much about this town. Do you know anything about a baby being born in this town around January 4, 2000? We've been told it was a miraculous birth."

The man perked up. "Yes, ma'am, I believe I do. You see, it was a night I will never forget. A young couple stopped in here. The woman was very pregnant. They needed a place for her to rest. The husband had tried everywhere in town, but because of the ice storm, all the motels and hotels in town were full. That wouldn't take much, we only have two motels and one old rundown hotel. I felt sorry for them and let them stay in the back room of my station. During the night, the woman delivered a baby boy. They stayed here until morning, then an ambulance took her to the hospital's clinic downtown for a checkup. That was the last time I saw them. They did sent me a Hanukah card. It came from Nazareth. I am sure that is where they live."

Reuben's wife couldn't believe her ears. Maybe this was the place.

"Is there anything more you can remember?"

"Oh yes, most definitely, there were two men and a woman from south of town. They were shepherds. The men said an angel appeared to them and told them to come to Bethlehem and seek a child who would save the world. They were to follow a star. Ma'am, it was cloudy. There were no stars. They came anyway and saw the star on my sign. It was glowing a bright red. Ma'am, that star hadn't been working for ten years. It was a miracle."

"Do you remember the couple's name?"

"All I remember is their first names, Joe and Mary. I think you could find out more at the hospital."

"Oh thank you, thank you, Mr.--?"

"George."

"Mr. George, you have been a great help."

Miriam sprinted across the street and told Reuben. He waved his crew and out to the local clinic they sped. Sure enough, a child was born in a gas station on January 4, 2000. He and his mother, Mary Feinstein, were checked in and subsequently released. They were from Nazareth. The clinic had their address at that time and a copy of the birth certificate.

Reuben could not believe their good fortune. He called Hiram, who was in Texas, and Rabbi John, in Oregon. They would wait for his call to see if their quest was over. Reuben and his crew drove to Nazareth. The weather was warm. They stopped at the address they were given. A little boy came running out the door. He was about three or four. He stopped at the gate.

Reuben asked, "Is your mother or father home?"

"Mommy's home. Dad is down at the new house he is building. He's a carpenter. I'm going to be a carpenter when I grow up."

"Would you go and get your mother, little boy?"

"Sure."

"By the way, what is your name?"

"Jesus," was the answer.

The boy ran inside and soon a young lady appeared carrying another child. She smiled as she approached Reuben.

"May I be of help?" she asked.

Reuben answered, "Ma'am, I'm Reuben Sachs. I'm an astronomer. Three years ago, I saw a phenomena in the heavens. It was a bright star. The next night it had disappeared. Through much research by my colleagues and me, we feel it was a sign of something significant. We feel a special child was born to save our world. Do you know anything about this?"

Mary smiled again and replied, "Yes, I do. You see, the boy you see running around here is our son, Jesus, Son of our living God. An angel came to me and told me I was to be His mother. I did not know how it will happen or when, but I know God has plans for His Son. We will just have to wait to see what they are."

Reuben knew he had discovered the child they had been looking for. He called over his crew and asked them to kneel.

"This boy, my fellow workers, is Jesus, the Son of God. Remember this day and this child, for some day he will lead us."

The crew took photos and recorded the words of Mary and Joe. Reuben called his friends and told them the quest was over and they should come and worship this wonderful child.

Both replied they would be there in twenty-four hours. The next day Hiram and John arrived. They fell down and worshipped both Mary and her son. The little boy giggled at the men on their knees.

"Please arise, my good men," said Mary.

"But this boy is to grow and be the leader of the world, Mrs. Feinstein."

"Yes, I know, but he still is a little boy and doesn't understand his future yet."

Hiram stated, "Mrs. Feinstein, my university is prepared to offer a full-ride scholarship to your son when he becomes of age. Just call the university any time before he turns sixteen."

Reuben added, "I will personally be his mentor through college without charge."

Rabbi John finished with, "The church will give you and your family $10,000 dollars per year until he is 21. We will also finance his entrance into any seminary he chooses."

"Oh, thank you, thank you. You have been most kind. Please stay until my husband, Joe, returns from the capital. He's working on a special project for the government. He'll be home tonight."

"We will most certainly wait. We want to meet the father—or is he a step-father of this wonderful child?"

"He is the father, since Jesus knows no other father yet."

The three scholars decided to stay at a motel with their entourage in

Nazareth. They wanted to discuss their next step. They also had to report to world headquarters in Jerusalem. There is an eight-hour time difference between Nazareth, Indiana, and Jerusalem, Israel. Reuben would call to report in the morning.

That night, before he called the headquarters in Jerusalem, an angel appeared to Reuben.

"Reuben, do not call Jerusalem. There are those there who want to harm the child. They have given you false statements. Go home by another route and let them be. They may find you and ask, but you are to say nothing about your findings. Maybe a little white lie will have to be told. The Boss said it would be all right just this once."
Reuben and his crew quietly left. He warned Rabbi John and Hiram Goldman the next morning. They were all in agreement.

The Jewish higher-ups searched for years for the child. Two years later, the head rabbi died and the threat for Jesus was nullified. The new church leaders were more liberal and accepted all new branches of Judaism.

Now, if this the way it happened, Jesus would be eighteen years old and learning his father's trade. In another decade, he would emerge as a religious leader and the world would change. The old guard would not disappear, but become an adversary of the new faith. They would persecute Jesus's followers, but the new way would prevail. Christianity would be born.

The Ghost of Bonner's Mill

She was seen many times sitting on her tombstone in the cemetery of Bonner's Mill, Vermont. When a man approached, she disappeared, but if a woman approached, she would become animated. She would smile, then raise her hand and point to a spot on the hill across the valley. She wore a sleeping gown and tiny slippers. Those who approached her tried to follow the line of her pointed arm. Across the valley was an old building which was built in the early part of the nineteenth century. It had been many different businesses, a general store, a drug store, a bar, and now a coffee shop called The Pity Pot. It was a place for artists and writers to meet. They would have their espresso drinks or lattes and tell each other of their troubles.

Why did the ghost continue to point toward the building? Why did she disappear when a man approached? What was her story? These questions were on the minds of Jean and Don Pershing when they entered the quaint town of Bonner's Mill, Vermont, a little town on the Kenebecasha River. It was a town which started with woolen mills, but the demand for Vermont granite grew and the quarry outside of town became the main employer.

Jean and Don checked into the town's only hotel. The room was small but very clean. The whole town was like going to a bed and breakfast for a stay. In the hotel's dining room, the locals gathered for their evening meal. Jean and Don sat at a front table. Everyone coming in could see they were newcomers. "Foreigners," the locals called them. Bill Harrick was the first to extend his hand to Don.

"Good evening, folks. I'm Bill Harrick, the mayor. What brings you two to this corner of the world?"

"I'm Don Pershing. This is my wife, Jean. We investigate ghost stories and ghost sightings. We do this for a hobby. We are both college professors at Warmack College in Virginia. We heard of a ghost named Stella Simpson. They told us there have been sightings of her in these parts. Do you know anything about her?" Don asked.

There were grumblings and quiet talk among the rest of the customers. They had had many of these so called "ghost busters" come and go. Actually, they were proud of their ghostly Stella, but they wished she would leave them alone. Her presence brought too many foreigners to town. Many tried to figure out the ghost, but none of them were successful.

"Do I? You betcha! Most everyone in this room has seen her once or twice. She hangs around her grave up on Cherry Hill Cemetery. All we know is she is there more often this time of the year. People have tried to approach her, but as soon as you get close, she disappears. Women seemed to get closer than men. She is always pointing across the hill. You should go see Ella Strom. She knows about as much as anyone. Ella claims she talks to the ghost, but I don't know if that is true. Ella is missing a few cards in her deck. If you know what I mean."

"Maybe she is the one we should see first. Does Ella live around here?" Jean inquired.

"Yeah, she is still around. She lives over at Country Gardens Retirement Home. It is just about six blocks from here on Oak Street."

"Do you think she'd mind talking to us?"

"Hell no, she loves to talk to anyone who will listen to her. Old Ella is 101 years old, but she'll talk for hours if you let her."

"Thank you for the information, Mayor. Jean and I will go see her tomorrow."

"Take some of the bakery's sugar cookies with you. She loves people who bring her sugar cookies and coffee."

"Thanks for the tip. We'll stop by the bakery before we go."

The next morning was bright and sunny. The Pershings headed for the bakery. They asked for six sugar cookies to go. The lady behind the counter smiled and asked, "These aren't for Ella Strom by chance?"

"Why, yes, they are. How did you know?" Jean replied.

"I also assume the Mayor told you she loved those cookies."

"Yes, he did. Is there a problem?"

"Ella hates sugar cookies. She likes chocolate chip cookies and from my bakery only. That Bill, he always likes to play tricks on outsiders."

Don interrupted, "Now who do we believe? You, or the mayor?"

"Well, I trust this lovely lady, but just to be on the safe side, let's buy a half dozen of each and let Ella choose. I'll eat the sugar cookies myself. They look delicious!"

Don and Jean had the cookies packed in a box with the sugar cookies on the bottom. They drove to the retirement home to see Ella. When they asked at the desk, they were disappointed to hear Ella had had a fainting spell and was in the hospital in Montpelier recuperating. She, however, planned on returning tomorrow. The receptionist asked why they were interested in Ella.

"We heard she knows something about Stella Simpson."

"She does. You see, Stella was Ella's mother. I'll tell her you were here. She'd be glad to tell her stories to someone else."

"We'll be back about one o'clock in the afternoon. Will that be a good time?"

"For her, yes. Most of the residents take a nap, but not Ella. She is a sharp little lady for her age. I'll have one of the aides make sure she is ready to talk to you."

The Pershings left the home and returned to town. Next stop, the town library.

"Do you have any old newspaper records here?" Jean asked the librarian.

"We do have some old microfilm of the town's former newspaper. It went out of business years ago, but we have papers that date back to the 1800s."

"The older the better. We're looking for references to Stella Simpson."

"Oh, so you must be ghost busters. We have a lot of people try to solve the mystery, but no one has come up with a good answer yet. That Stella, she is a sly one."

"Have you seen her?"

"Oh yes, several times. Most people think I'm just dreaming, but I have seen her on Cherry Hill many times. She always looks so sad. I'll go in back and get you all our film."

"Don, why don't you go to the city hall and court house and find what you can. I'll stay here and review these papers," bossed Jean. "Tonight we can go the cemetery and try to meet this Stella."

"Right on, I'll come back just before the library closes at five." Don answered.

Jean and Don ate their supper and spent some of the evening talking with the local residents.

"She comes out about 10 o'clock."

"Be careful and don't surprise her."

"Your husband should stay away. She hates men."

At nine thirty, Jean and Don made their way to the cemetery. They stopped about a block outside the gate.

"I'll stay here by the gate and watch," Don told her. "I don't want to scare her away."

Jean approached the hill and Stella Simpson's grave marker. Silently she waited in the shadows of the pine trees. It was after ten. Was she going to appear? Was this ghost story just a myth? *I'll wait until ten thirty*, Jean thought to herself.

She was just about to return to the gate when a faint light appeared next to the tombstone. It became brighter. Soon the figure of a young woman dressed in a sleeping gown appeared. She gazed across the valley. Jean cautiously approached. It seemed as if the figure wasn't aware of Jean's presence.

"Please don't be frightened," Jean spoke softly. "Are you Stella Simpson? May I be of some help?"

The ghost turned and started to fade.

"Please don't go. I only want to help you find the truth," Jean stammered.

Stella brightened. She pointed to the building across the valley. Jean followed her gaze and outstretched arm. It didn't point at the store front at all. She pointed at a large house just above the store.

"So, it's not the Pity Pot at all. Something happened in that old mansion beyond."

Stella nodded. She began to move. She motioned for Jean to follow. Jean stayed several yards behind. Stella moved to another tombstone. This one read, "Richard O' Brien, 1873 -1902." Then she flowed to a small stone. The grave was of a small child. It read, "Kathleen Angela Simpson. Baby daughter of Stella Simpson and Richard O'Brien. 1902, 6 days."

The ghost stayed at this little stone for just a moment as if she were weeping. She turned and looked at Jean. One more time, she motioned for Jean to follow. She flowed across the hill to a large, elaborate stone. It dominated the surrounding stones like it was king of the hill. The names on the stone were "Jessica Ann Morris, 1864 – 1908. Judge Howard John Morris, 1863- 1936."

She shook as she stood before the stone. She glanced at Jean, who was some five yards behind, and started to return to her original grave. She flowed swiftly as if she were late. Jean tried to follow, but was slowed by the trees and grave markers along the way. When Jean approached the Simpson grave, she saw Stella resting for a moment. Jean had to go behind a tree to get to the site, and as she came around the large trunk she found Stella had disappeared.

"Don, come up here. We have some work to do."

Don climbed the hill and said, "What did you learn? I watched as much as I could, but when you disappeared over the rise I lost sight of you."

"She took me to several graves. I want to take down as much information as possible before we leave tonight. I know where the stones are right now and I might forget by morning."

Jean and Don retraced Stella's path. They noted the location as best they could in the dark. They wrote down all the dates and names of the deceased. After an hour or so, they returned to their car and headed back to the hotel. As they entered the hotel lobby, the old clerk behind the desk asked, "Did you see Stella? Was it scary? I'm glad you're back so I can close up and go to bed."

Jean answered, "Yes, we met Stella. She is beautiful. Sorry we're so late."

"That's okay. I don't get time to watch the late shows very much. It was entertaining."

Jean and Don shook their heads and headed upstairs to their room. They would have a busy morning before going to see Ella.

The next morning, Jean returned to the library and Don made another trip to the courthouse. They had new names to identify and new stories to discover.

Jean found out that Richard O'Brien was an immigrant from Ireland. His parents died as the result of the Land War in Ireland. It wasn't a violent war, but his parents happened to be in the wrong place at the wrong time. They were caught between the two sides and were murdered. Richard lived with his Uncle Clarence until he was sixteen. He was alone when he came to America. The quarry outside of Bonner's Mill attracted him to find work there. He was involved in an accident at the quarry and was crushed to death.

The judge, Howard Morris, was a prominent citizen of Bonner's Mill. Not only did he rule the courts, but also the politics of the village. He, Dr. Silas Stone, and the county attorney ran the town.

Jean found out Stella's parents were murdered by a couple of thugs. Stella's father was the minister for the Episcopalian Church. According to the news article, no one was ever charged for the crime. The sheriff, Tom Dolan, and his wife took the poor little girl in and raised her for several years. Around the same time as the quarry accident, Stella was found guilty of being a prostitute. Judge Morris took pity on her and made her a servant in his home. His wife was ill and needed extra care. Stella filled that need. It was better than going to prison, but not much.

Don returned from the courthouse with copies of all kinds of documents. Birth certificates, death certificates, adoption papers, and court findings by Judge Morris. The two would have a busy day or two going over all the material, but it was lunchtime, and they were to meet Ella at one.

When they arrived at Country Gardens just before one, they were told Ella was waiting. The aide showed them down the hall to a sunny room at the corner of the building. There they found Ella sitting in her over-stuffed chair. She was a tiny person. The years had been kind to her, though. Her eyes sparkled, and she showed a big smile when Jean and Don arrived.

"Good afternoon. I hear you would like to know more about my mother, Stella Simpson. She's been the talk of the town for years. I wish she would settle down and go to bed like everyone else in the cemetery. What happened, happened, and she can't change it! Maybe you folks can change her mind."

"Well, we don't know if that is possible, but it has been said the reason ghosts hang around is that they are trying to tell us something. Oh, by the way, I'm Jean Pershing and this is my husband, Don. We are so pleased to be able to talk with you. It is rare to visit with someone who actually knew the deceased."

"Well, I'm glad to talk to anyone who will listen. Most think I'm daft. They think I am making up the story just to protect my ghostly mother. Pretty soon I'll be able to join her. I'm 101 years old, ya' know."

"We brought some cookies for you. We heard conflicting reports on which flavor you like so we brought two kinds, chocolate and sugar. Which do you prefer?"

"Chocolate chip from Betty's Bakery. Is that where you got them?"

"Yes, we did. You know the lady there said you preferred chocolate chip. I guess she was right. Do you mind if we record our conversation? We don't want to forget some important item."

"Heavens no, go right ahead."

"Okay, let's get going. You start when you are ready. Don will run the recorder."

Ella sighed and took a deep breath.

"My mother came to America from England with her parents. Her father, my grandfather, was an Episcopalian Minister. The church sent him over to minister to the people of southern Vermont. John Simpson and his wife, Anna, settled here in Bonner's Mill. The church was already built, so he just had to fill the pulpit. The story goes that grandpa refused to listen to the political powers in the town. Judge Morris, Dr. Stone, and the county attorney, Dewey Cheetem, had their own ideas on what should be said on Sunday morning. They wanted to keep the people afraid of them and the church.

"Grandpa and his wife lived in the parsonage behind the church. When Stella started school, she was teased by the other children because her clothes were so tattered and patched. 'Little ragamuffin,' they called her. They would push her down and grab her cloak to wipe the floor. Grandpa became so frustrated. He finally lashed out at her treatment in church on Sunday morning. The people applauded. He kept preaching about equality and abuse. He spoke of the treatment of the immigrants and those who could not read or write. He claimed some of the workers at the quarry were treated wrongly. Discrimination was rampant.

"One Sunday, he told of the corruption in the court system. He never named names, but everyone knew who he was speaking about. This outcry sparked action by the judge and his cronies. They first sent a terse message about sermons. He was told to stay with the teachings of the Bible and stay away from the town politics. Grandpa told the group he was preaching from the Bible. Jesus taught of love and justice for men. He assured them he would not back down. Of course, this was not what they wanted to hear. Two days later, a couple of bullies arrived at the parsonage. They beat up Grandpa. They tied up little Stella and her mother and locked them in a closet. They stole what few valuables the couple had. It was two Sundays before the Reverend could preach again. He hobbled up to the pulpit and looked out at the congregation. His eyes were on fire, as if they could penetrate everyone's soul.

"He said in a booming voice, 'God knows who did this to me and my Anna. I don't care if you beat me to death, but tying up and tearing the dresses of my lovely wife and my little girl is the last straw. I recognized the men who attacked us. Their voices and speech identifies them. They were men who work for Judge Morris and Dewey Cheetem. They are their thugs. They enforce the rules set down by the Judge himself. May the wrath of God Almighty descend upon their souls and smite them down.'

"Then he pointed his bandaged finger at the judge and exclaimed, 'You, Judge Howard Morris, should be ashamed of yourself. I declare the Devil himself will come to get you and take you to his lair. You will burn in Hell forever.'

"With that, he stumbled as he descended the steps. He caught himself on the pew occupied by Dr. Stone. 'And you, Dr. Stone will be right next to him in Hell. May God have mercy on your soul.'

"Anna got up and helped the preacher down the aisle. Stella followed closely behind. The congregation was stunned. As soon as he had cleared the door, Judge Morris approached the pulpit.

"'That man is a liar. I did nothing,' he exploded. 'I had nothing to do with hiring those two thugs who beat the pastor.'

"A voice from the back called out, 'Then how did you know there were two thugs that beat up Pastor John?'

"The congregation went deadly silent. The judge glared at the people. He stomped out of the sanctuary. Three days later, while the pastor and his wife were reading the Bible in the evening, the same two men broke down the door and forced their way into the tiny room. They grabbed Anna and started to tear her dress off. The pastor jumped one of them and began to hit him with his Bible. The man was huge and he tossed the reverend into the corner. His partner grabbed the man of God and held him while the other finished stripping Anna naked. He had his way with her. His partner, a much smaller man, took his turn. She lay on the floor bruised and bleeding. Pastor John got free for a moment and rushed to her side. My mother, Stella, was hiding quietly in the next room. She heard everything that was happening.

"'Anna, Anna, my lovely Anna. My God! What have they done to you?' he cried. He looked at the two men who were now grinning and joking about the incident. One of the men noticed the extra door leading from the room.

"'Hey, they had a little girl when we were here last time. Maybe we can split her, too. I'll see if she is in this room.' He laughed as he jiggled the door knob. He pushed it harder, but it wouldn't budge. He growled and worked on the door. The big man came over to the door and with one big kick the door flew open. No one was there. Stella had escaped out the window and was running into the woods. There was no sense in chasing a little frightened girl, so the men returned to the living room.

"The frightened pastor looked at the men and made one mistake when he said, 'I know you. You're Paul Finnegan and his younger brother, Sid. You work for Judge Morris at the quarry. I met you at Kelly's Store. You'll never get away with this.'

"'I'm sorry you said that, Pastor. You're not supposed to know us. Now we have to kill you and your wife,' Sid remarked. With that he pulled out a pistol and shot the minister in the head. He turned and looked at Anna. She screamed. He fired again and hit her in the chest. She fell forward over her husband.

"'Let's get out of here,' Sid hollered at his brother. They ran out the door and were never to be seen in Bonner's Mill again. But you'll find out later they did return and do some more dirty work for the judge.

"Stella waited for several hours before returning to her home. She feared the men would be waiting for her. When she did return, she found her parents lying dead on the blood-stained living room floor. She ran as fast as she could to the sheriff's home and pounded on his door. When the sheriff peeked out the small window in the door, he wondered why Stella was there. He let her in. She was frantic and crying. The sheriff's wife came downstairs and tried to calm her.

"'They killed my mommy and daddy,' she cried.

"'Who did?' said Sheriff Tom.

"'I don't know. A big man and a little man. The big man called the other Sid.'

"'Where are they now?'

"'I don't know. They ran away.'

\'"Let me get some clothes on and we'll go over to your place and see if we can find any clues. Mary, you hold Stella while I change. I think she needs someone to hug her right now.'

"After Tom had dressed, he grabbed his shotgun and went to the barn to hitch up the horses. He and Stella rode over to the little house behind the church. He could see through the window that the oil lamp was still burning on the mantel. He opened the door and went inside. There on the floor covered in their own blood was the most loving couple in town, dead. *Who would do such a thing? What was the motive? Tom thought to himself. Now what is little Stella going to do? The court will have to decide her fate.*

"He returned to the buggy and Stella. 'Let's go to my place for tonight. There is nothing I can do for your folks. We'll wait until morning and investigate more thoroughly.'

"Stella nodded. Even at her young age, she knew very little would be done in Bonner's Mill as long as Judge Morris was in control. In a day or so, the men who killed her parents would be far, far away. The judge would make sure of that.

"Of course, the town was shocked. Judge Morris vowed he would catch the scoundrels and bring them to justice. He went through the motions of drawing up warrants for their arrest. He blustered to Sheriff Tom about staying on the case forever. He claimed he would take care of little Stella himself. Sheriff Tom and his wife intervened and said they would take care of her. This pleased the judge because he really didn't want to be bothered with a little girl.

"Stella lived with the Dolans for the next seven years. She grew up to be a beautiful young woman. Her parents' death was never solved. They were buried in the back of the cemetery. Since there was little money in their estate, only wooden markers were used to identify the graves. Time and weather destroyed the markers in a short time, and no one really knows their exact burial site."

"You mean no one ever chased the thugs?" Jean quizzed Ella.

"No. Everyone knew that Judge Morris knew where they were. But he wasn't going to tell."

"Do you want to take a break, Ella?"

"Yes, I'm getting sort of tired with all this talking."

"Maybe we should come back tomorrow. We don't want to tire you. I may pay the cemetery another visit this evening. Maybe Stella knows where her folks are buried."

"Why don't you come in the morning? I'd love to go out to the hotel for lunch." Ella chuckled.

"It's a deal. I'll come by at ten. We'll visit a while, then meet Don for lunch. He can spend some time at the courthouse."

Jean and Don said good-bye to Ella and headed back to the hotel.

"Do you really want to go back to the cemetery?" Don questioned Jean.

"How are you going to get her to show you her parents' graves?"

"I don't know. Maybe she understands sign language."

"All right, but I'm going, too. I don't want you talking to a spook all by yourself. I'll keep my distance."

After a delicious dinner at the hotel, Jean and Don bid the patrons farewell and headed for the Hill. Jean waited patiently about twenty yards from Stella's stone. Dusk settled over the graveyard. At eleven o'clock, Stella reappeared. Jean approached the wispy figure. The ghost turned and faced Jean. Jean could tell she was troubled.

Jean spoke quietly. "Do you know where your parents are buried?"

Stella nodded.

"Would you show me where? I'd like to register it in the sexton's books."

Stella motioned with her hand. Jean followed her to a weedy, overgrown patch at the back of the cemetery. Stella knelt and traced two squares on the ground. Jean drew close to Stella. She knelt beside her. The soil felt cold inside the squares and warm outside the squares. Jean reached into her pocket and placed a small flag in the ground. Jean must have gotten too close. Stella bolted away and started to fade.

"Don't go. Please. I'm sorry I got too close," Jean pleaded, but Stella swiftly faded into the brush. Jean stayed on her knees for a while. Don approached her from her right.

"Are you all right?" he asked.

"Yes. I guess I came to close to her. I could feel her aura. I need to find out more. I did find the graves of her parents, though. I put some flags at the corners of the graves. See?"

"I see nothing."

"But I put them right here. Shine the flashlight over next to the brush."

"I still don't see them."

"She must have taken them."

"No, she didn't. There they are, over there by that mound. She must have pulled them and stacked them there."

"Well, I'll be. Never had that happen before. Guess it is time for us to go home, honey. Ella will be glad we found her grandparents' graves."

The next morning, Don dropped Jean off at Ella's. He went back to the courthouse to search records.

"Good morning, Ella. How are you doing? Are you ready for some more questions?"

"Sure am, and I can't wait for lunch at the hotel."

"I've got some good news, Ella. Stella showed me where your grandparents' graves are."

"Really? Do you think that will give her peace?"

"No, I think she has more to tell."

"Okay. Where did we leave off yesterday?"

"Stella's folks had just been murdered."

"Oh yes, now I remember. Like I said, Stella grew up to be a beautiful young woman. In Bonner's Mill, women were few and good-looking ones rare. One day a young Irishman, Richard O'Brien, arrived in town. He had come to Bonner's Mill for work. He had heard the quarries were hiring. He stayed for a while in the hotel, but soon found a rundown shack near the quarry as his place to live. At a Saturday night dance, he spotted the lovely Stella. He asked her to dance and walked her home that night. Soon he was courting her with flowers and gifts he really couldn't afford. They fell in love with the blessing of the sheriff. Sheriff Tom liked the hard-working Irish lad. But in quarry towns, there are rivalries, and fights between the Irish quarry workers, Italian stonecutters, and Welsh miners were frequent. Young O'Brien was involved in many. Several times, the fights landed him jail. Judge Morris noticed Richard's eye for Stella and didn't like it. He thought Stella should not be bothered by a low-class worker such as Richard O'Brien, especially since he was Catholic. No self-respecting Episcopal girl should consider a Catholic.

"Of course, love conquers all. Stella and Richard stayed together. Their passion became great. After a dance, Richard walked Stella to his place. She stayed all night. She crept home in the early morning hours. Sheriff Tom reprimanded her soundly. She apologized and said she would not do it again. But as lovers go, once the passion starts, it is difficult to stop. In October, Stella found out she was pregnant. Tom and his wife were disappointed but still supported her. On the other hand, Judge Morris was furious. He started a plan to split them up. Judge Morris spread stories about Stella that she was a whore and it was a crime to have a child out of wedlock. Richard begged the Judge to let him marry Stella, but the judge wouldn't hear of it. Judge Morris chastised the sheriff and his wife for not raising Stella up in a Christian home. He even threatened Sheriff Tom with the loss of his job.

"Soon afterward, there was an accident at the quarry where Richard worked. It seems he was placed in a very precarious spot to guide the huge blocks of granite. Somehow the cable broke and the stone fell on him. Killed him instantly. The sheriff investigated the accident and found the cable had been tampered with. Someone had cut some of the strands, making it weaker. At the hearing, the sheriff said nothing because he was afraid he would lose his job. What was a dead Irishman worth, anyhow?

"Of course, Stella was devastated. She was carrying his child. They buried Richard O'Brien on the hill. The judge brought charges against Stella for prostitution and took her from the Dolans. She was to spend time in the women's prison in Montpelier, but the judge made a deal with her. She could stay in town and have her baby as long as she lived and worked as a servant in his home. His wife was in poor health and needed extra care. Stella reluctantly agreed. Anything would be better than prison, so she thought.

"Judge Morris was mean. He worked her hard and his wife was always on her, saying she was lazy and stupid. Stella was about seven months along and feeling very tired. She sat down on the top step of the steps to the basement in the judge's house. No one knows if she became dizzy or if someone pushed her, but she fell down the stairs. The very next day, a baby girl was born prematurely. Today, they might have saved the poor little thing, but not then. The baby lived only a few days. Stella buried her next to her true love, Richard.

"Now the judge had accomplished what he had set out to do. Get rid of the Irishman and his love child. He still would not let Stella free. She was to be the nurse and maid to his ailing wife. There was no escaping. Judge Morris's wife, Jessica, became even weaker. Soon she was bedfast. Stella's work load increased. She would be done with her work about eleven and she would start again at six. Her little room off the kitchen was her only relief."

"Did she get paid for her work?" Jean butted in.

"No, remember, she was working out her sentence at Judge Morris's. Anything she wanted, she had to beg and plead for his mercy."

"You know, it is about lunchtime. How about we quit for a while and head for the hotel? Don will be here in a few minutes."

"Oh my goodness, how time flies! I'd better retire to the bathroom and get myself ready for the crowd at the hotel," Ella shot back.

Sure enough, just as they were about to go outside and wait, Don showed up. "If we get to the hotel early, we can pick the best table."

In a few minutes they were sitting down at the center table. Ella didn't want to miss greeting everybody. As the patrons wandered in, all of them had to stop and say hello to Ella. She enjoyed her meal and outing.

It was almost two before they left the restaurant. Both Don and Jean helped Ella back to her room. Before they could get seated, Ella began to continue her long tale.

"Wait a minute, Ella. We've got to get set up," Don said.

She paused a moment, then started again. "Now, where were we. Oh, yes. In Stella's room behind the kitchen. Well, one night after she had readied herself for bed, she heard a knock on the door. 'Stella? Stella? Are you dressed? It is me, Judge Morris.'

"Stella got up and went to the door. She slowly opened the door a crack. 'Do you want to see me, Judge Morris?'

"'Yes, I do." The judge shoved the door open. He looked at Stella standing there in her old nightgown, light from the lamp behind her showing through her thin garment. It showed her lovely curves and legs. Stella was shocked to see the judge. He had a funny look on his face.

"'I'm here to be with you, Stella. Take off your gown,' he told her quietly as he lifted his nightshirt over his head and stood naked before her. His ugly overweight body repulsed her.

"'No! No!' she screamed.

"'Quiet. You'll waken Jessie.'

"He put his big hand over her mouth before she could say anymore. 'Take your gown off. Now!' With his other hand, he grabbed her hair and pulled it back roughly.

"Stella nervously unbuttoned her gown and let it slide off her shoulders. He let her loose. She stood there in front of him, shivering and naked.

"'What are you going to do? Please don't hurt me,' she stammered.

"'Don't worry, my lovely Stella, I'll be gentle. Don't resist me!' he said as he shoved her down onto her bed. He raped her and left. Stella was shaken. She knew she could not run and the judge would tell everyone not to believe a whore. Poor Stella!

"This happened for several nights. It seemed to happen when Jessie had a bad night. Stella began to dread the knock at her door. It wasn't long and Jessie died. Now Stella was alone with Judge Morris every night. He came to her room many times. Of course, the inevitable happened. Stella became pregnant again. One day, when she was at Kelly's General Store, Hannah Kelly asked how she was feeling. Stella broke down.

"'I'm with child, the judge's child. I'm sure he will make me get an abortion. I don't want to go through that. What am I going to do? He'll deny anything,' she moaned.

"'My dear child, let me see what my George says.'

"In a minute, she returned with some good news. The judge would be going to Montpelier for some kind of a conference the next day. George said he had heard the judge tell everyone at the hotel.

"'I'll tell you what. I'll come over to the judge's place this evening and ask if you can come over tomorrow and I'll teach you how to make maple apple pie. He loves that flavor of pie. I'm sure he will let you come,' Mrs. Kelly told her.

"Stella went back home with a lightened heart, but what would Mrs. Kelly do for her once she arrived? That night the Kellys made a call on Judge Morris. He agreed to let Stella out of the house for one day.

"The next morning, Judge Morris left for Montpelier. He said he would be gone for three days. Ten minutes after he left, Stella hurried over to the General Store. Hannah met her at the door.

"'Hurry, the stage coach leaves in fifteen minutes.'

"'What stage coach?'

"'The stage to St. Johnsbury. There you will catch a train for Portsmouth, New Hampshire. Now hurry!'

"'But I haven't any money or clothes.'

"'I know. The town collected some money for your trip. I have some clothes stuffed in an old bag to get you there. You go to Miller's Café when you get there. My sister and her husband run it. They will take good care of you. You may have to work some, but nothing like the torture you've had to endure at Judge Morris's. Now go!'

"'But, but what about you? The judge will certainly be upset.'

"'I'll just tell him you ran off with a tramp and the last I knew, you were headed for Boston. Remember, you're a whore. That's what he calls you. Don't worry about me. I can handle that S.O.B.'

"'Why, Hannah, I'm shocked, but thank you, thank you. I'll write.'

"'No, no. The judge will discover where you are. I'll keep in touch with my sister. Now hurry.'

"Stella hurried to the stage line and boarded. She took one last look at her prison on the hill for one the last time and smiled. She was free at last.

"When the judge returned, he was furious. He sent two of his cronies off to Boston to retrieve his fleeing slave girl. Of course, she was already in Portsmouth and safe. Mrs. Kelly made another call. This time it was to the best friend of Howard Morris, Dr. Silas Stone. She explained Stella's plight, but was careful not to reveal Stella's whereabouts. He was astounded. He knew the judge was crooked, but for his own sake and his reputation he kept quiet. This was more than he could allow. He confronted the Judge. The judge denied his accusations. In fact, when he was threatened to report the judge to the judicial board, the judge countered with how he would reverse the doctor's malpractice suits. Still Dr. Stone pressed charges. An investigation ensued. The judge was relieved of his duties. He was not put in prison for his many crimes because of his stature in the community and because many of the persons he had sent to prison were still there. He plea-bargained with the board. He'd not cause any problems if he could only live out his life in Bonner's Mill. The judge was a broken man.

"Stella became a waitress at Hannah's sister's restaurant. She had her baby and that was me. Stella lived in Portsmouth for several years. Judge Morris died. A few days after his death, a letter came from Hannah. Stella was named in his will. She would receive notice soon. Sure enough, two days later a letter from a judge in Bonner's Mill requested her presence at the reading of the will. My mother and I returned to Bonner's Mill. At the reading, she found out she inherited all of the judge's estate: his house, his quarries, and all his money. She was a rich lady.

"We lived in his house for the rest of our lives. I married the banker's son and we moved in with my mother. The house was so big, there was plenty of room for all of us. Many summers she would return to Portsmouth and work the café, just for something to do. She claimed she missed all those folks who helped her. She died at the age of 98 in 1990. We buried her in a quiet service next to her first love, Richard O'Brien. Ever since then she has been scaring folks by not going to bed. I hope you can solve her problems."

"Boy, that's quite tale. Oh, my gosh. It's four thirty. It is time for you to go to dinner, Ella," Jean remarked.

"Oh, that's okay. I've been late before, but I am getting a little tired from all this visiting."

"We'd better go. We'll see you in a couple of days, Ella. We have to research this story some more. I believe we can give your mother some rest."

"That would be nice," Ella answered.

Jean and Don left Ella in the dining room with her friends and returned to the hotel.

At dinner Jean and Don discussed the last couple of days.

"Which one of the many issues do you think Stella can't free herself of?" Don asked Jean.

"It could be the death of her first child? It could be trying to tell everyone about the cruelty of Judge Morris? Maybe it's the death of her parents? That was never officially solved. I really believe it is the accidental death of her true love, Richard O'Brien. Judge Morris definitely had a part in his death. I think we should pursue that course. If we can find those old hearing records and prove Richard was murdered and his death wasn't accidental, I think we can put her to rest. You know, I'd like to visit the big house she lived in. She pointed her hand toward the house the first night I met her."

"Do you really think that is smart? What will you find out there? The place has been abandoned for years. Let's go to Montpelier and search the archives," Don suggested.

"No, I believe she will come to the house if I'm there alone. Come on, honey, you're not afraid of ghosts. Are you? We have one more day before we have to go home. Let's say good-bye to Ella in the morning and spend the rest of the day at the Historical Society."

"Sounds like a good plan. Now let's get to bed. I'm beat," Don commented with a sigh.

"You go to bed. I'm checking out the old Simpson house. Maybe Stella will be there."

Don rolled his eyes. He knew he would have to let Jean go and he would worry until she returned. Jean sensed his anxiety and said, "I'll be all right. I've got my cell phone. If I need you, I'll call."

Don headed up to their room and Jean quietly walked down the street to the Simpson house. Originally it was Judge Morris' place, but Stella and her family had lived there so many years that the name changed. Jean stood a moment at the yard gate. It hung by one rusty hinge. The sidewalk was overgrown and the grass needed mowing. Bushes and trees covered most of the downstairs windows. The glass in the upstairs windows had either been broken by children throwing stones or the frame had rotted away. In one window, a ragged piece of drapery fluttered in the breeze.

The house was a full three stories and had a huge wrap-around porch with fancy gingerbread trim. One of the steps cracked as Jean stepped up the four steps to the porch floor. Jean flicked on her flashlight as she approached the front door. The door was slightly ajar. It groaned as she pushed it open. Inside was furniture covered with dusty sheets. Cobwebs were strung from corner to corner.

Jean made her way through the parlor to the dining room. The huge table was covered in dust and fallen plaster. Chairs were in their place as if waiting for someone to come for the next meal. Jean wandered around the first floor until she found a doorway leading to the back or servant stairs. She cautiously climbed the rickety dark stairway.

At the top of the stairs was a long hallway. The first door was shut. Jean tried to open it. It seemed locked. She gave the door a slight kick. The rotted frame splintered and the door opened. Inside was a little room with a single bed and small dresser. Jean slowly crossed the floor to the bed by the window. As she gazed through the broken glass, she could see Cherry Hill Cemetery across the valley. She thought she could see a faint light on the opposite hill.

Is that Stella? she thought. *Does she know I'm here?*

Jean sat on the small bed. It creaked under her weight. She turned out her flashlight and waited. The wind, though slight, moaned through the house. It was so quiet. Jean could hear the mice scampering across the floor. She was about to leave when the hall brightened. She went to investigate and just outside the door was Stella. Stella pointed to Jean and shook her finger as if to say, "Jean, do not enter this room."

Jean quickly exited and started down the stairs. She didn't want to offend the ghostly figure. The door to the little room slammed shut. As soon as she reached the bottom step, Stella reappeared. She motioned Jean to follow.

Jean stayed a few steps behind the floating figure. Stella pointed to a door. She wanted Jean to open it. Jean turned the knob and the door creaked open. It led to a stairway to the basement. Jean was about to go down when Stella floated in front of her, blocking her way. Stella moved to the huge fireplace in the front of the house. She pointed to a brick on the side of the face. Jean touched the brick. It moved. The brick was loose! Jean carefully removed the brick. Behind it was a chamber containing a small tin box. Jean looked at Stella. The ghost seemed to want Jean to remove the box.

Jean slid the box out. It had a hinged lid. She opened it and inside was a newspaper clipping. She slowly and carefully unfolded the newsprint. She grabbed her flashlight and turned it on. As quickly as she turned it on, she turned it off; she had forgotten about Stella. It was too late; the ghostly Stella had disappeared. Jean refolded the news article and placed it in her purse. Then she replaced the box in its chamber and replaced the brick.

Jean spoke to an empty room. "Stella, if you are listening, I now know the room at the top of the stairs was your room where the judge raped you, the stairs are the ones you were pushed down, and the brick is your secret. I'll take care of the article, Stella. Really, I will. Thank you. Thank you."

There was a loud crash outside. Jean jumped and turned to run. Outside she found Don cursing the broken step.

"Are you all right, honey?" she asked.

"I was just coming to say the same thing to you," he replied. "Did you see Stella?"

"Yes, she showed me her secret. Hurry, I can barely wait until I can read it. Let's go back to the hotel."

They returned to their room. Jean spread the newspaper article on the desk. Although yellowed and faded with age, the print was still legible.

"May 3, 1902. The investigation into the untimely death of Richard O'Brien was dismissed by Judge Howard Morris for lack of evidence and therefore ruled an accident.

"The court also found Stella Ann Simpson guilty of prostitution on two counts and was sentenced to one hundred eighty days in the state prison. The Honorable Judge Howard Morris had mercy on the poor woman and suggested she work off her sentence as his housekeeper. Case closed."

"We have to get to Montpelier and find these court proceedings," Jean exclaimed with determination.

The next morning, they went to the retirement home and said their good-byes to Ella. They promised her they would return next year during spring break. Ella assured them she'd be waiting for their return.

Jean and Don spent the winter researching the archives and old newspaper accounts of anything related to Stella Simpson. Once, in early March, they returned to Montpelier to search in person. The staff at the records department was very grumpy. They had seen ghost busters before and digging into old files and records was time-consuming and dirty. The only reason they consented was because the law said they had to.

The legislature was in session and the search was delayed. Jean and Don continued to badger the employees. They also found some records of Stella's existence in Portsmouth. It wasn't until spring break that they had a positive breakthrough. While thumbing through some old files titled Court Records of Belknap County, a worker discovered the hearing of Richard O'Brien, dated May 3, 1902. She called Jean about her find. Jean told her to save it for them because they were to arrive in Montpelier next week.

When investigating the precious folder, the Pershings discovered evidence that was disallowed by the judge. The judge was the one and only infamous Judge Howard J. Morris. He had disallowed Sheriff Tom Dolan's testimony on the grounds that he, the sheriff, was biased and unworthy of presenting factual evidence. Much to Jean and Don's surprise, the statement made by the sheriff was not destroyed, but merely not allowed in the judge's decision.

Jean scanned the handwritten report. Sheriff Dolan reported he had evidence that the cable supporting the granite block had been tampered with. He also stated the regular operator of the crane was not at the controls on the day of the accident. Sid Finnigan, one of the judge's lackeys, was at the controls. It seems the regular operator was beaten severely in a fight the previous night. The sheriff's report also stated that Richard O'Brien had been moved from a position at the top of the quarry as lookout to a position at the bottom. He replaced another man who had also been involved in an altercation with two unknown assailants.

The whole hearing was a scam. The judge had set up the murder to make it look like an accident and refuted any testimony which might suggest otherwise.

There were also documents stating Stella Simpson was a prostitute and she was working illegally in a shack by the quarry. It stated the Honorable Judge Howard J. Morris showed pity on her and took her in as a housekeeper instead of sending her to prison.

Don took a copy of the document. He asked if the courts of Vermont ever reviewed old court cases.

He explained Stella Simpson's daughter was still alive and she would be relieved to find closure and justice for her mother.

"Isn't that the ghost everyone talks about over at Bonner's Mill?" the associate remarked.

"Yes, I guess she is famous in the state of Vermont."

"I'll talk to the attorney general and see what she says."

"That would be wonderful. Do you think there is a chance?"

"I think. We Vermonters like to have justice served, even if it is a hundred years late."

Within the next week the Attorney General replied. She was going to review the case and would present it to the Court of Appeals. Jean and Don were elated.

"We must go and see Ella and tell her the good news," Jean told her spouse.

When they returned to Bonner's Mill, the town was already abuzz with the news. They were surprised to find everyone knew about the find.

"News travels fast in Vermont. Somebody always knows somebody in Montpelier," stated the mayor. "Now, with the internet, we are really fast."

The mayor paused for a moment and said, "I'm sorry for the attitude of this town and for my trying to trick you with those sugar cookies. It's that we have so many people showing up and making fun of us. You are the first couple who really stuck to the mystery. I truly hope you can give our famous ghost some peace."

The Pershings visited with Ella and told her it would be a waiting game.

"That's fine with me. I've got plenty of time," laughed Ella, "When you're my age, time means nothing. You know, I'm going to be 102 in June. Are you coming to my birthday party?"

"You betcha. We'll be here," Jean answered with a smile.

It was June before any news came from Montpelier. One day an official looking document arrived at the Pershing home. Inside was the review of the hearing held by the Court of Appeals of the State of Vermont. They found Judge Morris negligent in his dealings on the case of Richard O'Brien. There was probably enough evidence to convict the now-deceased judge of murder along with his accomplice, Sidney P. Finnigan. Unfortunately, all parties involved were now deceased, so no action will be taken except to charge the person involved with the crime and change the report from one of accidental death to one of suspected homicide.

The next day Jean and Don made plans to return to Bonner's Mill. As before, the townsfolk knew all about the ruling. They were on hand when Jean and Don entered the hotel.

"Do you think this will make Stella happy?" asked the mayor.

"I don't know, but in a few days we will try and find out," Jean answered. "First, we have to talk to Ella. We heard she is having a birthday party tomorrow."

"That's right. It is going to be at the town hall at noon. A lot of the folks from the home want to come, too. So they scheduled the party in the daytime. She'll be glad to see you."

The birthday celebration was a success. Ella was surprised to see Jean and Don. When they told her of the court ruling, she said, "Well, now I can die. Nobody believed me but you young folks. I know my mother will be pleased. Have you told her yet?"

"No, the weather is not been right for cemetery prowling, but I think to tomorrow it is supposed to clear. She doesn't usually appear this time of the year. I hope she makes an exception for me."

"I'll see what I can do. I talk to her daily, ya' know," Ella snapped back.

It didn't clear for two more days. This was unusual weather for the time of year. Finally, on Friday, the sky cleared. The moon was full. Jean and Don ventured to the Hill. Jean slowly walked up the slope to Stella's grave. Don followed several yards behind, trying not to be seen. As Jean approached the stone, Stella appeared. She looked at Jean, and then she looked past Jean to Don. She motioned for both of them to come forward.

Jean said very softly to the figure, "We found out your fiancé was murdered and he did not die as the result of a quarry accident. We also discovered Judge Morris was involved. He hired the killer to make it look like an accident. The man he hired was Sidney Finnigan, the person your father named before he was murdered. We also feel the judge pushed you down basement stairs and caused you to lose your first child, Kathleen, but we cannot prove that. Only you know that. You can rest in peace."

Stella nodded as if to say "Thank you." She turned toward Don and nodded to him also. Don answered and told her it was a privilege to know her. She pointed at the old Simpson house still standing across the valley. Just recently it had been condemned and was to be torn down. She stretched out her arm and waved her finger as if casting some kind of a spell over the building. Her form became ultra bright, as if on fire. A small ball of glowing matter passed from her finger. It flew across the valley toward the old house and disappeared.

Stella swirled away from them and flew over to Richard's grave. She knelt and kissed the ground. Out of the grass another figure appeared. The two of them embraced and as they embraced, both of them became more visible. The pair knelt beside the next grave. Stella lifted a small object from the ground. It was their baby, Kathleen. The two lovers stood there holding the ghost child.

A laugh came from the direction of Judge Morris's headstone. There he stood in his judge's robe, all pompous and proud. Stella turned and pointed her arm at the huge stone. Fire as a lightning bolt flashed, but there were no clouds. It was as if the bolt came from below the ground. The stone split down the middle and crashed to the ground. The ground opened and a loud moan came from the judge. It sounded like, "No-o-o-o!" Then a scream echoed as if someone were falling into an abyss. The ground closed back and he was gone.

The three figures stood close together with their arms around each other. Their aura started to glow. It became brighter and brighter. Soon it seemed as if they were floating off the ground. They passed close by Jean and Don. Stella reached out to Jean and brushed her shoulder with her fingers. Jean felt nothing but the warm feeling of letting someone go. The ghostly figures rose higher and higher through the pines. Suddenly they paused, as if waiting for someone. Stella reached out, beckoning someone to come.

Soon a small light appeared. It came from the hill just outside of town. It became larger and larger. First it looked like a young girl, then a young woman, and finally a mature woman. Stella and the new arrival hugged. The group, now numbering four, turned toward Jean and Don. The last figure to arrive blew them a kiss before the ghostly group started to rise again. Don and Jean watched as long as they could. Soon the celestial family became just one of the many stars which dotted the sky and they were gone.

Jean and Don stood there mesmerized by the scene. They were brought back to reality when they heard the fire sirens wailing in the distance. Across the valley the old Simpson house, the house Stella lived in for so many years, was in flames.

Did Stella start the fire? There was no one living in the structure. How could it catch on fire? Don and Jean knew, but they were not going to tell. They hurried back to town and watched the mansion burn to the ground. It was going to be demolished anyway, so no effort was made to save it. The volunteer firemen just made sure no other buildings were in peril.

The next morning, Jean and Don made their way out to see Ella. They were stopped at the reception desk by the chaplain.

"I'm sorry to tell you this, but last night, about the time the fire alarm went off, Ella died quietly in her sleep. We know it was after the fire alarm because she had pushed her emergency button. We checked in on her. She wanted us to get her some of her heart medicine. We did and left her asleep. We found her this morning when she didn't come down for breakfast. I'm so sorry. She loved you folks dearly. May God rest her Soul. She was a delight to know all these years."

"This is tragic but prophetic. She waited until someone proved her story about her mother and her mother's lover, Richard. When it was done, she, too, had done her part. Now they are all together in Heaven. I know it!"

Jean and Don stayed for the funeral. They received many compliments on their work.

"You can come back any time you want," explained the mayor. "The gates of the town will always be open that is if we had gates."

"Thank you, Mr. Mayor. We will get back as often as possible. We've made many new friends here and we feel Stella will not be present anymore. Tomorrow we must return to Virginia, so this will be good-bye until we meet again."

Wolfpack

It was a cool July morning in the North Carolina mountains. Charlie Wright admired the trees along his path to his dock on the Warrenville Reservoir. The water was smooth with a light fog covering the glassy surface. The morning sun would soon dissipate the fog. It was going to be a great day for the old Korean War vet. He reached the dock and picked up his fishing pole.

As he sat down in his lawn chair, he noticed a pink object in the water about ten feet from the dock. He looked again. It was a body, floating facedown in the water. He grabbed a rope with a weight on the end and threw it over the body. He pulled it to the dock.

It looked like a young woman, but her head was shaved. The bald head had something written on it. He couldn't make it out. Charlie secured the body to the dock and hurried back to his shack.

He was out of breath as he talked to the dispatcher at 911.

"This is Charlie Wright. I found a body floating off my dock in Warrenville Reservoir. I need the sheriff to come right away."

The voice at the other end tried to calm Charlie, and she assured him she would send someone out.

Sheriff Joe Wagner overheard the message as it came in. He was very new at his job. He had been with the department for several years, but as a deputy only. The previous month, a scandal broke in the sheriff's office. Even though Sheriff Tom Schafer had served the county for sixteen years, he was part of the scandal. Charges were filed by a woman detainee. She claimed a deputy fondled her and forced her to strip. Sheriff Tom quickly fired the deputy in question, but the deputy, who was charged, told a local reporter t he whole story. He claimed Sheriff Tom Schafer was also involved in the sexual harassment. Good ol' Sheriff Tom video-taped the harassment for his pleasure. The deputy provided tapes and DVDs of the events to the press.

They showed strip searches of young women who were picked up for minor offenses. The prettier you were, the longer and more intense the search. The women complained, but Tom trumped up the charges to make the searches plausible. Of course, the searches were done by male officers. Sheriff Tom had no women officers because he felt women were not capable to serve as law officers.

The sheriff and the deputy were charged and the case went to trial. The deputy was given five years on probation and Sheriff Tom plea bargained and was let off, but had to resign. Joe Wagner was appointed interim sheriff until the November elections.

The first action Joe took was to hire a female officer. Out of several applicants, Jill Johnson seemed most qualified. She had trained as a MP at Camp LeJune Marine Base. Her tour of duty was over and she decided to return to civilian life.

The new sheriff and his new hire, Deputy Jill, drove out to Charlie's. Both of them figured Charlie was having hallucinations. His time in Korea was not pleasant and he was prone to seeing things.

Charlie met them in his drive and led them to his dock. Sheriff Joe was shocked. There was a body. He and the deputy tugged the body toward shore and turned it over. It was a young woman, all right. She was wearing only her underwear and her head was shaved. Across the top of her bald head was written "rabbit." Joe radioed for help and the coroner.

He had the office check missing persons. The report came back as he suspected. She could be Cindy Connors of Taylorville. She hadn't returned home from the state baseball championship game in Raleigh, which was against the Warrenville Wolves. Taylorville defeated Warrenville 5-4 in 10 innings. She'd been missing for four days. It turned out she was the girlfriend of the relief pitcher who struck out the other side in the ninth inning and won the game. They took photos and statements. The body was transferred to the county morgue for positive identification.

Joe walked out on Charlie's dock and surveyed the reservoir. It was a fairly large body of water. The surface area covered 20,000 acres. Because it was considered a private lake owned by the North Carolina Power Company, the shoreline was not controlled by the government. The power company sold many shoreline properties to private individuals. There was approximately forty miles of usable lakeside. This side of the body of water was lined with several cabins and small boat docks for a mile upstream.

Charlie's home was the last cabin before the dam. The power company wouldn't sell anything closer. Across the lake were three cabins, Jonas Smith's, Doc Walton's, and a vacant cabin soon to be torn down. The power company decided to yield to public demands and gave the rest of the shoreline to the state to use as a park. The park had a campground and a beach.

Joe studied the water. He would check out each cabin on this side and have Jill go to the campground and check to see if someone heard anything. The park ranger kept a list of campers. All those camping in the park four days ago would have to be contacted. The maps of the water current would also be investigated. It had been known to many that trees and branches on the north side somehow drifted to the south side before coming to rest against the water intakes of the dam. There were four intakes for the dam. Two supplied the water for the turbines and two were to control the depth of the lake.

Joe and another deputy checked each cabin and its occupants on the south side. Jill researched the north side. When she interviewed several campers about the previous Friday evening, they told her they had heard what they thought were wolf howls followed by a woman's scream. It came from the direction of Dr. Walton's cabin.

Sheriff Joe looked at the bulletin board. They didn't have much to go on. Was the girl a crime victim, or was it case of teenage stupidity? But why the shaved head with the word rabbit scrawled across the top? Things didn't add up.

In the middle of November, another body was found floating in the backwaters below the dam. She was a young black woman. She was wearing only underpants with her head shaven. Her bra was entangled around her neck. She evidently had passed through one of the intakes. On the top of her head was written "doe." It turned out she was a girlfriend of the young man who ran for the winning touchdown against the Warrenville Wolves two weeks before.

The sheriff was perplexed. Both women had no signs of abuse except having their heads shaved. The feet of the last victim were scratched and bruised as if she had run on stones and rocks barefoot. When they discovered her, her lungs were filled with water; therefore, she drowned. Probably she was knocked unconscious when she hit the surface and didn't recover. It proved she was alive when they hit the water. Why, who, and where were questions Sheriff Joe would have to figure out. He soon discovered it was Vonda Jenkins from Hobert High School. She went missing two night after the game.

After the second death, Joe decided to call the North Carolina DCI. He needed help. This was bigger than his department could handle. The DCI sent a young lady, Peg Palmer. She was a blond and very statuesque. Her luscious smile was deceiving. Beneath the warm exterior was a hardened cop. She always wore slacks and a jacket that concealed .38 revolver. She was well trained in the art of self-defense. She and Jill made a good team.

She discussed the two cases, and her analysis gave it different slant. She realized the drowning came after a defeat by a Warrenville sports team. This would indicate either a fan or some high school students who sought revenge for the losses. Peg told Jill she was assigned to the case and anytime something new came to light, she would come immediately.

Nothing happened all winter. Most of the cabins along the reservoir shore were closed. The basketball team of the Warrenville Wolves tied for the conference championship with the Millersburg Marauders. Jeremy Shellsburg of Millersburg team hit the winning shot at the buzzer. Warrenville was denied the crown.

Joe was concerned the defeat might cause another mysterious drowning. He doubled the patrol around the reservoir. Nothing happened. He relaxed the patrols the first of May. It looked as though the revenge theory was not applicable.

Later in May, the night of the Millersburg prom, Jeremy and his girl, Shelly Williams, ventured out to the lover's point at the state park. They were alone. A black van pulled alongside them. Three men got out and grabbed his girlfriend. They blindfolded her and forced her into the back of the van. Two others held Jeremy and placed cotton pads over his eyes and secured them with surgical gauze. They tied Jeremy with plastic rope and locked him in the trunk of his car.

He was found unhurt the next morning by the park ranger making his rounds. The surgical wrap was the first real clue they had. It must have come from a hospital or doctor's office. Joe and Jill headed for the Walton cabin. No one was there. There was evidence of some kind of party, but nothing indicated foul play. Joe stopped at the doctor's office on the way back. The doctor had little time for the officer, but he did indicate his son and some of his friends stayed at the cabin a couple of weekends ago. He also agreed to let Jill and Peg Palmer from the DCI search his cabin.

Peg arrived the next day from Raleigh. She suggested Jill interview the doctor's son and any others who might have been there. Maybe they heard something or had seen something. Jill contacted the doctor for his permission to interview his son, Dan. She stopped one evening at the Waltons'. She wanted his parents to be with their son.

She asked Dan, "On the night of May 17, did you hear anything coming from the lake and surrounding woods?"

"No, ma'am, I didn't hear anything unusual. Me and my friends had a bonfire and roasted wieners."

"Would you tell me the names of the others?"

"It was just me, Chad Harmon, and Cecil Dusenberg. I don't know if they heard anything or not."

Jill got the addresses of the other two young men. She thanked Danny for his information and left. She returned to the office to find the sheriff still there.

"What did you find out from the doctor's son?" he asked.

"He gave me the names of two others. I'll try to contact them." She paused for a moment. "Something tells me Danny wasn't telling me everything. He seemed nervous. But maybe just the interview with a cop made him nervous."

Jill interviewed Chad and Cecil. Their stories were similar. Chad did admit they had a few beers, but that was all. No one got drunk.

Six days later, a pair of fishermen discovered the body of a young woman in a cove about half a mile from Charlie's shack. She was semi-nude and her head was shaven. On the top of her bald head was written "fawn." The body proved to be that of Shelley Williams, the missing prom queen.

Peg was notified and she came immediately. She asked Shelley's parents if she could have an autopsy performed and blood drawn. They agreed. The autopsy and her blood proved Shelly had had no alcohol and she did not have any internal injuries, nor was she sexually molested.

The sheriff now had some clues. The pattern was young women, heads shaven, no signs of physical or sexual abuse, and all from schools that had previously beaten the Warrenville Wolves in some sporting event. It must be someone from his own town. He also knew it was a gang of three persons, maybe five. He warned the surrounding town police and sheriffs. The next significant loss by the high school team, everyone was to be on alert. He recommended all young women be escorted to and from school functions. No women should walk or drive alone until this crime was solved.

It was late in the evening. The 911 dispatcher received a desperate call came from a mother in the little town of Hoopes. It was ten miles north of town. A pair of young women was missing. They were supposed to be home by seven. They had gone to the mall in Warrenville. She wanted the sheriff to check the parking lot for their car. It was a light green VW, license EQ784. The dispatcher first called Sheriff Joe as the woman had asked. He was, of course, in bed at the time. He told her to call the Warrenville Police. It was their jurisdiction, but he would come down anyway. The police checked the parking lot and, sure enough, they found a light green VW with the right license plates. It looked like an abduction. They contacted Joe. He said he would meet them there in twenty minutes.

At the scene, they found the girls' purses in the back on the floor and they didn't appear to be touched. There was a slipper under the car. It indicated there was a struggle. Tire marks on the pavement showed the escaping vehicle left in a hurry. The girls's names were Amanda Toyne and Stacy Green. Joe needed to interview the parents quickly. The dispatcher gave him the phone number of Mrs. Howard Green. He called. She was distraught, but thankful Joe would come at this late hour.

The little town of Hoopes had no police as such. They relied on the sheriff's department of Warren County. Joe hurried to Hoopes. On the way, it began to rain. He received a bulletin. Deputy Jill had found two young women, bound and gagged and blindfolded, standing in the middle of the town square in Hoopes. They were wearing nothing but underpants. They were scared and very cold. Their names were Amada Toyne and Stacy Green. Jill was taking them to one of the parent's homes.

Joe arrived minutes later. The girls were wrapped in blankets and drinking hot chocolate. He asked if they would answer some questions.

Amanda started out. "Stacy and I had just finished shopping at the mall. It was 6:30. We were to be home by 7. I parked my new car away from the other cars in the lot. I didn't want to get a ding on it. As Stacy and I walked toward my car, we noticed a black van with dark windows coming toward us. We started running. I got my keys out and unlocked the door. We just had the door open when the van stopped in front of my car. Four men dressed in black hooded sweatshirts jumped out. They grabbed Stacy first. I ran over to her. They grabbed me also and made us get in the van. One of them took our purses and our shoes. I guess they threw them back in our car ."

Stacy butted in, "They made us sit on the floor and put our hands behind our backs."

Amanda continued, "We rode for several miles. The men in the back tied and blindfolded us as we went. We pulled into a barn. They told us to get out. They led us blindfolded to another vehicle. It was a pickup. We were put into the back on a mat. One of the men rode back there with us. We rode for a while again. The next stop, they pulled the mat out on the tailgate with us on it and told us to get out. We went through a door to a shed. They re-tied our wrists to some kind of a lift and raised it up. I could hear the motor running. We were back to back hanging from the lift. Our feet could barely touch the floor. The men laughed and teased us. Then one said because I am chubby and Stacy is skinny, they would call us Pig and Weasel. Next we heard them laughing and kidding each other. 'Pigs and weasels don't wear clothes. Let's cut them off. They proceeded to cut our clothes off, everything except our underpants.

It started to thunder and rain. The leader, we think, said, 'We can't chase pigs and weasels in the rain. Let's mark them rejects and send them home. First, we need to do the shaving. We were told to get down on our knees and not move. They retied our hands behind our backs. I could hear some clippers. Stacy started to cry. They were cutting off her long black hair. Next it was me. I could feel one of them writing something across the top of my head. The leader told us to get up, they were taking us home. We were placed back into the truck and the next thing we were standing in the middle of town in the rain. Our hands were tied, we were told to stand back to back while they tied our ankles and our waists. They removed our blindfolds, and we found ourselves standing naked in the middle of Main Street. That's when Deputy Jill found us. That's about it. Do you want to add anything, Stacy?"

Stacy said, "I heard one of them refer to themselves as a wolf pack. Otherwise, nothing more."

Joe thanked the families. He knew now it was someone from Warrenville. Probably a small gang called the wolves. He would relay the information to Peg. He was thankful the two girls were found alive and not drowning victims. What perplexed most was, if it was a small gang, why didn't the women show signs of sexual abuse? The only thing the "gang" did was shave their heads and strip them. They were too smart or too young.

He was just going to call Peg when his phone rang. It was Peg. She had heard the police bulletin and was on her way. She'd be there in an hour. Joe and Jill were to meet her at the Walton place. Jill had been up all night and Joe most of the night. Still, duty called. They met Peg at the locked gate of Doc Walton's. Joe had the code on the lock to let them in.

The trio drove slowly up the drive, looking for any sign of action. The lane was washed clean by the heavy rain the night before. Any tracks were washed away. In the yard was parked a blue and white pickup with Virginia license plates. Jill wrote them down and called the office for a check. Nothing in Virginia was open this early, so they would have to wait a couple of hours. Peg approached the back door. She knocked. Nothing! She turned the door knob. It was unlocked. She and Joe stepped inside.

Joe hollered, "Anybody here?"

There a shuffling of feet and a young man dressed only in undershorts appeared in a doorway.

"What do you want?" he asked sleepily.

"Are you Danny Walton? asked Joe.

"Yes."

"I'm Sheriff Joe Wagner. This is Peg Palmer from the North Carolina DCI. We'd like to ask you some questions.

Danny realized he was standing in front of a woman with only his undershorts on. He tried to cover himself. Peg just smiled and said, "Young man, why don't you get dressed. Then we can talk."

"Yes, ma'am. I'll tell the others to do likewise."

"Others? What others?" she quizzed him.

"Chad and Cecil stayed overnight with me."

"By all means, we would like to talk to them also. We'll wait right here."

All three young men appeared in ten minutes. Joe and Peg could hear them talking in the bedroom. Jill came in and reported that all the pickup had in it was some fireworks. The boys must have made a trip to Tennessee.

Joe and Peg questioned the three about the previous night. Their stories were the same. One mentioned they went through Hoopes. It was strange because Hoopes was not on the road to Tennessee. Joe thanked the boys left and told them to be sure and have one of their parents around when they shot off those fireworks.

Megan Tyler was a destined to be a premier swimmer. She had set many records at Warrenville High. She held the state record for the 800 meter and the 400-meter free style. She had a full ride scholarship to North Carolina University. In town, she was assistant manager at the pool. After work and on her days off, she would go to the high school pool and practice alone.

The football team was starting their fall practice. First it was just once a day, then twice a day. After football practice one afternoon, two of the players looked in the swimming pool door. They saw Megan doing her laps. They entered and stopped at the edge of the pool. Megan stopped when she reached the end.

She spoke. "Hi! What can I do for you?"

"Oh, nothing. I'm Chad and this is Cecil. We came in to watch. How far can you swim?"

"I do fifty laps every other day. I have to be in shape for the swim team at UNC."

They chatted a bit and the boys left. Two days later, Chad entered the pool room. He sat in a deck chair and watched. Megan ignored him although he was specimen of a good-looking male. He had blond curly hair and a body which reminded her of the statue David by Michelangelo. His muscles bulged underneath his sleeveless T-shirt.

She finished and he was still there. Today, because of the previous encounter, she wore her racing suit and not her usual bikini. She climbed out of the pool and began to towel off. Chad came over to her. He smiled nicely. His eyes were focused on her breasts. Megan looked down. Her nipples were making little mounds in her suit. She quickly wrapped the towel around her upper torso.

Chad asked, "Would you go to a movie with me tonight?"

Megan turned him down by saying she was supposed to babysit her niece. He thanked her and said maybe some other time. The next week, Chad came in every time Megan was practicing. He stayed until she was done. They would chat and he would walk her to her car. He seemed nice enough.

Megan decided to do a little research on the he-man named Chad Harmon. She asked around. She found Chad was a senior and the star quarterback for the Warrenville Wolves. He was a force to be reckoned with. He would let one believe he was Mr. Nice Guy until the second or third date. Then he became a monster. He kissed, mauled, and prodded each girl. He was inside her blouse or up her skirt, if she was wearing one. He had roaming fingers and could unzip, unhook, or unbutton a girl's garment in seconds. Although he was never accused of being intimate with any girl, he just liked to undress them to see if would look embarrassed, or make them run naked beside him. He would drag them along by their arm. In time, he would tire and stop. He would slowly give the girl back her clothes, one piece at a time. He would then threaten his victim by saying he would spread all over school the news to other boys that she was "easy".

One of Megan's swim team friends, Sharon Willis, met with Megan and explained her experience with "Mr. Macho". They met at the state park by the reservoir. Sharon had Megan's old job as life guard for the beach. They both knew of the isolated bench on Duffer's Point. There they could talk and not be disturbed.

Sharon started out, "One warm evening, Chad and I went for a walk in this park. I'd been dating him for about a month. I'd just gotten off duty. You know I was the envy of the girls at school."

"Yes, all the girls thinks his is a stud."

"We walked to the far end of the park where it was densely wooded. We stopped in a little clearing which looks over the lake. You know the one where it drops off about forty feet to the water. I must admit I was scantily dressed. I'd been on the beach all day in the sun. I was quite warm. All I had on was shorts and a halter top. All of a sudden he grabbed me by my upper arms. He told me he wanted to see me naked. I tried to scream, but he quickly held his hand over her mouth. He told me again to strip. Of course, I refused. He reached into his pocket and pulled out some kind of an animal shocker. He said he would use it me if I didn't comply. I shook my head, no. He placed the instrument on my bare leg and buzzed me. I must have jumped up a foot. Boy, did that hurt. He told me a third time to undress or he keep doing the shocking. I said okay. He let me back away onto a rock protruding over the water. I could go nowhere but jump onto the rocks below, so I stood silently really not ready to undress in front of him. He smiled at me and pulled out his cellphone. He held it up to take pictures of me. "Okay". he said, "Go ahead, I want to tape this. If you continue to stall I'll give another reminder." I started with my shoes, then my shorts. I stalled. He waved the shocker. I slipped my halter over my head and held it next to my chest. "Give me that and your other things." he ordered. I handed him my clothes. All I had on was my bikinis "All the way, my little sexy girl." he ordered. "I definitely want you in my collection." I took my bikinis off and stood there naked on the rock. He held out his hand to receive them also. I asked when I could have my clothes back He just laughed. He wrapped them around a rock and threw them far into the lake. This is the strange part. After he threw all my clothes away except my tennies, he laid his phone on the bench. He took off his shorts, which I found out was all he was wearing and stood naked in front of me. "Come here." he said. I thought he was probably going to rape me right there, but no. He picked up his phone and with a big grin he snapped a selfie of him and me. He looked at me one more time and picked up his shorts and left. "So long," he said, "I had a nice time. The gang will really like this video. Hope you get home okay." I was stunned. I must have stood there for ten minutes before I started to walk naked home through the woods. It was more than five miles. Lucky, I knew the back alleys as I got closer to home. I did pass by Mrs. Olson's place and her lights were on. I thought about stopping there, but she'd spread the wrong rumors all over town. I think I made all the way home without anybody seeing me. Boy, was I getting chilled. Thank goodness, my parents weren't home, so I didn't tell them. Thank goodness he didn't put on his Facebook page."

Megan wasn't surprised by the story and she believed Sharon. Sharon was afraid to go to the police, fearing the courts would not believe her. Chad's dad was a prominent citizen of Warrenville. He would protect his boy, who was destined for a good college scholarship. The courts would probably call it a childish prank because he did harm her. Chad would just receive a warning and a slap on the hands. Megan thanked Sharon for her update and promised she'd be careful.

The next day, Chad appeared again in the pool room. He asked for a date. Megan refused.

"What's the matter? Ain't I good enough for you?" he snapped.

"Chad, I'm going to be frank with you. I don't see any reason to become involved with you. I'm going to college in a week. You are here in Warrenville. Why don't you date the girls in high school? I'm just not interested."

Chad snorted. "Well, goddam. I thought I was being nice. Well, piss off, big Chapel Hill swimming star. I hope you drown."

With that, he stomped out of the pool room and slammed the door.

Megan was glad, but also worried. What if he came back? He didn't return again the next week. On this particular day, she was not scheduled to work until six. She told her mom that she was going to school for practice. It was daytime and she should be safe. She pulled on her suit at home and covered it with her sweat and t shirts as she drove over to the high school. She swam for an hour or so.

The coach of the football team stopped by to say he was leaving. Did she know how to lock up? She told him yes. When she finished, she went to the girls' locker room to dress. She hated wearing her wet suit under her sweats. She always brought dry clothes with her, but Chad's intrusions prevented her changing fully sometimes . She peeled out of her suit, and showered. She had a funny feeling in her stomach while she stood there in the big shower room all alone. It was as if someone was watching her. She shrugged it off as silly and dressed in a T-shirt and sweatpants. She grabbed her car keys and wallet from her locker, and headed out the janitor's door. She could see her car was the only car left in the lot.

While crossing the parking lot, she noticed a black van driving toward her. She hurried her pace. It came faster. It drove up beside her car. She reached into her purse and tried to find her can of pepper spray, but she was too late. Three men wearing black hooded sweatshirts got out and grabbed her before she could find it or open the door to her car. They forced her into the back of the van. She was forced to lie on the floor, facedown. One of the men kept his foot on her back. They were laughing about their catch. This would be the best.

"Hometown women are better than the others," they chortled.

Megan recognized the voices. The driver was Chad Harmon, high school quarterback. The man riding shotgun was Danny Walton, the school geek. His dad was a doctor for the town.   There was one they called Ted. It must be Ted Horner, basketball player. The other two remained a mystery for a while. Megan felt her phone vibrate in her pocket. She tried to slowly pull it out.

It was her mother. No one noticed. She began texting without looking.

In the van, Cecil caught her using her phone.

"She's texting," he screamed.

"Get it away from her."

"Hand it to me. I'll throw it out the window. Nobody will ever find it."

Cecil grabbed the phone and handed it forward. Danny tossed it out the window.

"What do you suppose she texted?"

"Who cares? She's ours now."

The van turned many corners. Megan figured they were doing it on purpose to throw her off. Finally, the van pulled into a shed or garage.

She could hear another vehicle starting.

"We're going to move you," said one of them.

They sat her up and blindfolded and gagged her. Her hands were tied in front of her. They led her from the van to the back of a pickup. Two of them picked her up and slid her inside the bed of the truck. One climbed in with her. They loaded some cases of something along side her. She heard the doors shut on the cab and down the rough road they went. The truck growled along. It stopped. Someone got out. The truck moved ahead. That someone got back in.

"Did you put the sweeps on the back?" someone asked.

"Yeah, and I made sure there were no tracks leading off the pavement."

The pickup growled up a steep incline, then coasted. Megan could hear the gravel cracking under the tires.

Back in town, Megan's mom was getting worried. Megan would be late for work. She phoned her husband, Fred.

"Megan is late. She is practicing at school. Could you swing down there on your way home?"

"Sure, honey. I'm sure she just forgot about the time. You know how she can swim forever," he reassured her.

He drove into the school parking lot. Megan's old Dodge was there. She's just swimming overtime. I'll go in and stop her, he thought.

As he pulled up to her car, he noticed the door was open. He got out. Her wallet and keys were on the pavement. One of her flip flops was under the car. She was nowhere to be found. He called her name and got no answer. He dashed to the school building . The door was locked. He peered in the big window at the end of the pool and could see it was empty. There were no light coming from the locker room area. Megan was not there. He dialed 911.

"This is Fred Tyler. I think my daughter may have been kidnapped. Send someone right away. I'm at the high school parking lot."

The sheriff and police arrived quickly. They searched the area and her car. The kidnappers had not taken any money or jewelry. Her laptop was still in the front seat. The only thing missing was her cell phone.

"Have you tried to call her?' asked the sheriff.

"No," answered Fred.

"Try her and see if she answers."

Fred dialed his daughter. They waited.

Fred received this text on his phone: "kidnapd. 5 gys. Luv u. call."

That was all. The sheriff was excited. Maybe he had found the missing piece to the drowning s. He didn't want to alarm the Tylers, but it was five guys who kidnapped the Williams girl. It was five guys who kidnapped the two young women from Hoopes.

Sheriff Joe contacted the cell phone company. Could they pinpoint the call? They claimed they could get within 500 yards. Joe took Fred's phone and headed to the area designated by the phone company. It was on a blacktop road leading around the north side of the lake. He spread the deputies out along the road. He dialed. The phone rang. One of the deputies yelled, "I hear it."

They converged on the road bank. In about ten minutes they found the phone. Now Sheriff Joe knew what road to check.

"Check every cabin drive along this road," he ordered.

Molly and Fred Tyler went on TV and begged for the safe return of their daughter.

Time was critical.

The pickup carrying Megan continued on the gravel lane. It stopped and let some passengers out. They slammed the doors. She could feel the truck backing up. The tailgate opened. Two men pulled the mat she was lying on out to the tailgate. They helped her to her feet. They told her about how far she would be going. Her bare foot hurt as she walked on the gravel. She tried hopping on her sandaled foot. Soon she was walking on grass. Being blindfolded, she could only guess at the distance.

"Stop!" said Ted's voice. "Cecil, open the door. Megan, there is a step up. Raise your foot now ."

She was led into a room. Her hands were untied and leather wrist gauntlets were tightened on each arm. She could feel them being hooked to some kind of a chain with a bar attached to it. Ted removed the blindfold. When her eyes adjusted to the dim light, she found she was in a shed. The bar she was attached to was a boat hoist. The walls were covered with life jackets and anchors. This was a boat shed. There was a dim florescent light over a bench.

She looked down and saw she was standing on plush carpet. Cecil removed her remaining flip flop. Now she was barefoot on the carpet. Everyone left except him. He started at her neck and felt down her back and side. He pulled her sweats away from her body and looked inside. He continued down her legs.

She heard him holler to the others as he went out the door, "Piece of cake.

T-shirt, bra, sweats and panties. Dannycan handle this one. Let's get started."

She stood in front of the crossbar of the hoist, her arms and hands in front of her, but spread apart. She could hear them laughing and joking. The big overhead door opened. The five guys had transformed. They now wore wolf caps that covered their eyes. Two had T-shirts and the others were bare chested. They all had on breech cloths tied at the sides.

As they walked around her, she could tell that underneath they had on shorts or swim suits. They all had hanks of hair attached to their front panels. The hanks were blond, black, and brown. One was wavy, long, and black. They would flip the hair up as they pranced around. Cecil turned on the hoist and raised Megan to a standing position with her arms above her head.

Chad was the first to speak. "This is our first fox. She can swim. Therefore, she is a swamp fox. Has anybody here ever seen a swamp fox wearing a T-shirt?"

They all answered, "No!"

"Then we shall remove it. Dan, will you do the honors?"

Dannystepped forward and with a pair of surgeon's scissors. He cut up her sleeves to her neck, then he started at her belly and snipped slowly up the front of her chest. He pulled away the fabric and held it high. He ran to the fire and threw it in the flames.

When he returned, Chad asked if foxes wore sweats. The answer was the same. Dannysnipped up one leg and the other. He cut the waistband and the pants fell to the ground. He took them to the fire and tossed them on. The fire leaped. Sparks flew.

Megan was in her underwear and humiliated. This was sexual harassment plus torture of her mind. She had to watch as Danny returned. His eyes and face grinned with anticipation of more to come.

Megan thought to herself, *"Will they continue? Certainly, this where they quit. The other girls had their underwear on. Right now it wasn't any worse than a bunch of guys ogling a woman in a bikini."*

Chad was glowing. He asked, "Has anybody seen a fox wearing a bra? Should we cut it off?"

Only two responded with a yes.

"You mean, Ted and Jake are saying no. Then it is a tie vote. I get to break the tie. I say yes. Danny cut off her bra. Let's see some tits."

Danny stepped forward. He was about to snip when Megan brought her knee up into his groin. He doubled over in pain.

Chad reached for the hoist controls and raised Megan up until she was on her tip toes. He reached for a rope on the bench. He roughly tied one end to Megan's ankle and then looped around a bench leg. He motioned for Cecil to do the same on the other ankle.

"Now pull, Cecil. Spread her wide so she can't kick."

Megan was now in an almost spread-eagle position. Cecil let the hoist down so she could touch the ground.

Chad screamed, "Give me those scissors. I'll do the job. Kick my buddy in the nuts, will you?"

He cut her shoulder straps and, frowning at her, cut the fabric between her breasts. He pulled the bra away, scraping his hand roughly across her right breast. She stiffened in pain. Her face was at the same level as his. He looked her in the eye and belched a terrible beer-laden belch. She turned her head away in disgust. He smiled.

"I'll show what it feels like to be kicked in the nuts, you bitch. Just because you're some college star doesn't mean you are any better than me," he snarled.

He bent down and started to cut her bikini underpants. He stopped and grinned. He put the scissors inside the band on her right leg. He squeezed the handles. Snip! Off went one side. The other side hung helplessly on her hip. He cut the other side. Megan squirmed with humiliation. Chad caught her underwear as the fell away. He paused just a second.

"Now, my little vixen, you can run free as a breeze." Chad dangled her panties out to the side. "Here, Danny boy, let's watch these hot pants really burn."

Danny grabbed the garment and ran to the bonfire .

Now Chad had Megan naked with her arms stretched high above her head. It was all she could do to stand on her toes.

"My, my, what a nice body. How about a kiss?" Chad hissed.

Megan shook her head.

"Well, I'm going to anyway."

Megan hung like an animal ready to be gutted. Her eyes filled with terror. She writhed in her gauntlets. Chad grinned as he touched her lightly. He started at her lovely brown hair, then moved down her neck. He slowly massaged her breasts, pushing each one together then apart. He continued down her torso. He stuck his tongue out and made circles around her navel. He placed both hands on her knees and slowly inched them up the inside of her thighs to her crotch. He stopped and looked at Ted.

"Gimme those scissors, Ted. I want to clip off some of her pussy hair. I never had any pussy hair before."

Chad was getting nasty from too much booze. Ted held the scissors away and said, "No, you've done enough. You said we weren't going to hurt her because she's a hometown girl ."

Chad made a grab at the scissors. Ted flipped them to Jake. Jake tossed them outside into some bushes. Chad cursed the both of them.

He turned back toward Megan. He glared at her hanging there.

He growled, "I knew I had a good reason to spread your legs, bitch!"

Megan shook her head no. He pinched one of her nipples between his fingers. She stiffened in pain.

"I said, spread your legs wider, bitch, or I'll tear this little nipple right off."

Megan complied. He shoved his hand up between her legs and grabbed her flesh. He pinched and twisted her skin. She screamed, but it was muffled because of the gag in her mouth. Her back stiffened and arched. Tears flowed profusely.

"That's enough, Chad. Get out of here," Ted hollered at him.

Chad snorted and said, "You two chickens get her ready for the shearing. I'll be back with Dan."

He left with Cecil to join Danny by the fire. Jake quickly ran for the hoist controls and reversed the lift motor. He let Megan drop to her knees. Tears streamed down her cheeks. Ted released her wrists gauntlets so she could hold herself. Her right breast was red from Chad's rough treatment. Chad and his lackeys returned.

"So you let her down," he snarled at Ted.

"She was hurting and you said we were not going to hurt her. She's a local girl."

"Okay, you wimp. Now tie her hands behind her back. We have to finish the job. Take out the gag, too. No one can hear her scream anyhow."

Ted and Jake refused to tie her hands again. Cecil and Danny had to do it as she knelt with her head down. She was whimpering and sobbing.

"Quit your whimpering, woman. Oh, that's right, you're not a woman anymore. You're a swamp fox, a vixen. I've never seen a vixen with long brown hair. Has anybody hear seen a vixen with long brown hair?"

Danny and Cecil chorused, "No."

"What about you two or are you turning chicken?"

Ted and Jake stood silently. Chad took the clippers off the bench and showed them to Megan.

"Here, Dan, she kicked you in the nuts. You get the first cut."

Danny gleefully grabbed the clippers. He started at the back of her head and clipped right over the top, removing a large hank of hair. He grabbed it and danced around, holding it high. Chad was next. He ripped through her hair, almost pulling it out instead of cutting it. Megan cried out in pain. Chad chuckled.

Next was Cecil. He was a little more gentle. Ted followed Jake. He trimmed the last of her hair off neatly. She was completely bald. Chad grabbed a black marking pen and wrote "swamp fox" across her bald head. He took a mirror and shoved it in front of her face. She sobbed some more.

"You now are a swamp fox. Wolves like to catch foxes, especially vixens. Now, my little vixen, we have a deal to offer. We'll set you free. You can run as fast and as far as you can. If we catch you, you must go to bed with each one of us. I want you to sign this paper saying you agree to these terms."

"What if I don't sign?" asked Megan.

"We will have sex anyway. I hope you survive. The fire is hot. We will burn you until you submit," Chad answered. "Dan, go and fetch a burning stick. I'll burn this bitch's tits if she doesn't sign."

Danny ran to the fire and came back with a small log with hot coals on the tip. Chad grabbed it and held it close to her breasts.

"Now sign or I'll burn those little tits of yours."

Her hands were untied and she signed the paper. The thought of burning terrified her. Chad roughly pulled her to her feet.

"We'll give you a five minute head start," he told her.

"Don't I get any shoes or clothes?"

"Nope, foxes don't wear clothes. Foxes don't have long, brown hair. You go barefoot and naked like all the animals. Now get! The clock is ticking."

Megan ran out of the shed. She looked for an opening in the bushes. On the backside of the fire was a small opening into the woods. Megan followed the path. There were several cutoffs, but she knew they led to the cliff. She tried a couple, but the thorns and branches cut her skin.

She could hear the wolf gang yelling out the time. Three minutes! Two minutes! Then a loud yell, "Here we come".

The path got steeper and rockier. It cut the bottoms of her bare feet. The half moon lit the water of the reservoir. She could tell it was as smooth as glass the way the moonbeams shone on the water. Suddenly the right side of the bushes fell away. The left side rose up steeply. She was at the Wall. It was a 200-foot sheer wall of granite. It originally was 250 feet, but the water from the reservoir covered the bottom 50 feet. There was a narrow path about 50 feet up. It was a starting point for rock climbers. It ended about the middle of the wall.

The path narrowed to about four feet. Megan stopped to listen for the boys behind her. She could see the lights from their flashlights cutting the dark path. She had to continue. She had to hope she could find the path to the top and freedom. Up the steep path she climbed, until there was a flat outcropping. The path stopped. All that was left was the cliff protruding over the water.

"So this is what happened to the others. They were running in such a panic, they didn't see the edge and ran right off the cliff." she thought. The impact of the water either knocked them unconscious or knocked the wind out of them. If they didn't know how to swim, they were goners.

Megan stood at the edge. It was about 50 feet to the surface. Megan had jumped from the ten-meter platform at UNC. It was scary. This would be twice as far.

A light shot up the path. Megan plastered her body against the rock wall. She tried to hide. The light came closer. It spotted her and someone came running. The person started the light at her feet and slowly proceeded up her body.

"My, my, what have we here? A naked fox. Were you trying to hide from Dan? I found you and I get you first. Isn't that nice? Come out, little vixen. The wolves are waiting. Hey, guys, I found her. Up here on Lover's Leap."

Soon all five of the gang were training their lights on her. She stepped out toward the edge of the precipice. Her white skin shone in the bright light.

"Well now, we caught you. Now you have to pay. You lost. We won. So come off the rock to our den, my pretty vixen. The fun is just beginning. You sure have small tits, don't you?" laughed Chad.

"M-m-m-may I ask a question?" Megan stammered, trying to shield her eyes from the glare.

"Why sure. Wh-wh-what do you want to know?' Chad stammered back, mocking her.

"After you rape me. What then?"

"We're not going to rape you. Don't you remember? We gave a chance to escape and if we caught you, you consented to have sex with all of us. It would be consensual sex. No crime committed."

"You mean you will set me free afterwards."

Danny interrupted, "We can't free her. She knows all of us. She'll get us for kidnapping and sexual harassment and what about the others?"

"Shut up, Danny, she doesn't know about the others," Chad barked back.

"But Chad, what are we going to do with her? We can't just take her back to town. She has no hair. People will start asking questions. She can't stay here. I knew we shouldn't have got a local girl," Ted whined.

"Let's worry about what to do with her after we have our fun. I can't wait to bang this bitch! If all fails, I'll tie an anchor to her feet and take her out in the reservoir. Nobody will ever find her. I found a pistol in the drawer under the bench back at the boathouse. We can shoot her out on the lake."

"That's murder. I'll have no part of it," Ted stated firmly. "We are not doing that. I'm leaving."

"Okay, go, you yellow wolf. That will mean more time for each of us."

Ted turned away and ran down the path.

Jake followed him. He, too, was through with the Wolfpack.

Chad shouted at them, "You two don't leave here alive."

He fired the gun in their direction. Ted felt something hit his thigh. It was like fire. He reached down and his hand was full of blood. He couldn't see in the dark, but he could keep running. A second shot rang out. The fleeing pair could hear the bullet whiz by their heads and hit a tree. The third shot caught Jake in the shoulder. He fell. Ted stopped and lifted him to his feet.

"We can't stop, Jake. I'll help you."

Ted heard another shot ring out. He could hear it whistling through the trees. He dragged Jake down the path to the pickup. Jake was losing consciousness. Ted slid him in the rear seat. He removed their headgear and breech clothes. He hobbled to the clothes bin and exchanged their clothes. He found a belt and tied it around his thigh to stop the bleeding.

Sliding behind the steering wheel, he fired up the old truck. When he got to the gate he knew it was locked, but each side was just a wooden fence. Ted gunned the truck around the gate opening and smashed the boards. He reached the gravel access road. Instead of turning back toward Warrenville, he turned right. Within a mile the road ended at Highway 8 going to Titusville. Ted drove as fast as he dared, because he was fading in and out of consciousness. He veered off the shoulder several times. At last, he could see town lights.

The truck coughed. Ted looked at the gas gauge. It read empty. There was a convenience store ahead. Could he make it? The motor died.

Ted put the shifter in neutral. He rolled into the convenience store lot. The truck rolled into the concrete abutment protecting the pumps. Ted collapsed over the steering wheel.

Inside the store, the night manager thought it was probably some drunk and called the police. When they arrived, an officer tapped on the window. He got no response. He opened the door. Ted fell on onto the pavement. He was covered with blood. Jake moaned in the back seat. The officer called for help and an ambulance. Soon the two young men were in the emergency room at Titusville Hospital. While searching their belongings the police identified the boys. Jake was immediately taken to surgery. Ted was conscious and started talking. He told the police about the gang and the striping of the women. He said nothing about the drownings.

They called Warrenville police and the sheriff's office. It was four a.m. when the Titusville police called the sheriff's office. There was only one officer on duty plus the 911 dispatcher.

"Sheriff, I have two young men here in custody. Jacob Burns and Ted Horner. Do you know them? Mr. Horner has confessed to numerous crimes. "

"I'm not Sheriff Joe Wagner. I'm Deputy Tom Stillman. I'm the only one on night duty. I will call the sheriff, though. He gave us all specific to call him at any sign of a break in this case ."

Joe was sound asleep when the phone rang.

"Hello," he answered quietly. He didn't want to disturb his wife. She had just put in a long night with their colicky two-month-old baby.

"Joe, this Tom, down at the office. I just a call from the Titusville Police. They have two young men in custody. They have both been shot and are in the hospital there. Their names are Jacob Burns and Ted Horner. Do you know them? They will hold them there until they hear from you."

"I'll be right down. This may be our big break."

Sheriff Joe knew both young men, but he couldn't think of why they were in Titusville and wounded. When he got to the office, he called the Titusville Police. They traced the pickup by its license to a man in Virginia. Maybe he could help unravel the puzzle. The owner was traced to a Donald Burns. He was called by the Titusville Police. He verified the truck was his. He had lent it to his nephew, Jake Burns, several months ago.

"The two young men, are they hurt bad?" asked the sheriff.

"The tall one had a shot go through his thigh. The other one was hit in the shoulder and lost a lot of blood. His is in emergency surgery at the present. We will keep them here at the hospital until I hear from you."

"I'll call their parents and send a deputy to Titusville with them as soon as possible. Chief, I think we may have solved this nasty thorn in our sides. I'll call you back in a few minutes."

Back on the cliff, the remaining Wolfpack members confronted Megan.

"Now, our little vixen, let's get going. I can feel your warm legs already. My dick is ready," snarled Chad in his vulgar locker room language.

Megan stepped closer to the edge of the rock. She measured the distance.

"You say you'll free me, Chad, but you don't dare. I figure you would rather drown a defenseless fox than set me free. Here I am naked, no hair, and yet you are afraid of me. Sorry, wolves, I'll take my chances with the fishes."

With that she took two quick steps and dove off the cliff. The flashlights followed her descent. Her white skin reflected the bright lights.

She hit the water in less than five seconds. It seemed to her like an eternity. Her swimming knowledge took over. She clinched her fists so she wouldn't break her fingers on impact. She hit the water at 30 miles per hour. The dive took her deep into the water.

She curved her body upward and swam underwater as far as she could while holding her breath. When she surfaced, she was fifty yards away from the flashlights. One of the lights found her. Chad squeezed off his last two shots. She heard the bullets hit the water some twenty feet behind her. They were close enough. She took a quick breath and dove. She swam underwater for another forty yards. She stopped, caught her breath, and treaded water. She watched the lights pan the water, but they were far away from her.

Soon the guys decided to leave. Megan tread water and watched as they descended the path. She was safe for the moment. She glided out in the water and around an outcropping of rocks and trees. There was a cabin on the shoreline. At the dock there was a sign, "The Waltons". She swam to the dock and was about to shout out when she heard voices. It was the Wolfpack, returning to the fire. They were laughing and shouting.

"Dan, did you get some good pictures?"

"Did you get one of her hanging from the hoist? I'd like to post that one on the internet. I can see it now, Megan Tyler, North Carolina super swimmer, baring it all."

"Did you get one of me shaving her head?"

Danny answered affirmative.

"Let's see them."

"What about Ted and Jake?" asked Cecil.

"They are probably stranded on the road somewhere. The gas tank was about empty. I wouldn't be surprised if they aren't walking home right now," Chad chuckled.

"Do you think they will squeal on us?"

"Not a chance. They are a guilty as we are. Quit worrying. Come on, Dan. Show the pictures."

The lights in the cabin dimmed. A huge screen on the wall lit up. Megan crept out of the water and onto the lawn. She could see the screen clearly through the big picture window. The show started. The Wolfpack trio laughed and hooted at the photos of her hanging from the hoist.

"Show us some of the old photos, Dan," someone called.

He flipped on some photos of young women. They were in varying stages of undress. Megan watched with horror. These were the women who had drowned in the lake. They were all stripped of their clothing and made do to humiliating things. Now she knew why they ran away so fast and didn't see the cliff.

Cecil turned and looked out the big picture window.

"I see something in the front yard," he said.

"Go out and check. Who'd be here this time of night?" said Chad.

Cecil went to the door. Megan crept back down the lawn and hid in some cattails near the shore. Cecil flashed his light around. An old raccoon scampered across the porch. He laughed.

"Get out of here, you son of a bitch," he yelled.

As soon as he returned inside, Megan slipped back into the water and swam away. She could see a light across the reservoir.

She thought to herself, I *'m a distance swimmer. I'll head for that light. Someone has to be there. I will swim, then rest, then swim some more. I can make it* .

She began her five-mile trek across the lake. She kept her focus on the light. It was early morning when she arrived at the dock with the light bulb burning. She pulled herself up on the dock and collapsed from exhaustion.

When she awoke, the sky was starting to brighten. She sat up and looked around. There was a shack about 100 yards up the slope from the dock. Was there someone living there? She found an old jacket hanging on a post. She put it on and sat in the grass at the edge of the dock. She laid back and dozed again.

A slamming screen door awoke her. The sun was shining. She quickly threw the jacket on the dock and slipped back into the water. She hid behind some reeds. An old man with a white beard appeared. He stepped on the dock and removed his jacket. Underneath he was wearing shorts and a tank top. He did some jumping jacks, then sit ups and then pushups. Megan watched and smiled. The old guy was doing his exercises. The water seemed colder now than when she was swimming. She was shivering. She had to get moving. She took a chance and swam out about 30 feet in front of the dock without him seeing her. He was engrossed in his workout.

Treading water, she turned to face him and said, "Good morning, sir."

Charlie almost fell off the dock. He looked at her and said, "Who are you, boy?"

Megan replied, "Megan Tyler, and I'm not a boy."

She swam closer to where the water was shallow and stood up. The water came to her waist. Charlie reached for his glasses.

"I'm a girl. May I come in and sit on your dock?" she asked.

"By all means, young lady. What happened to your hair?" he said. "Say, aren't you the girl they are looking for? Are your parents Mollie and Fred Tyler? They were on the TV last night."

"Yes, I am. They cut my hair off last night."

"Who's they?" he asked.

"The wolf pack. It's a bunch of guys from town."

Charlie helped her climb onto the dock. Megan stood quietly and began to shiver. Charlie took one look at the beautiful mermaid who had appeared. He grabbed his shirt and wrapped it around her shoulders. Megan grabbed him and hugged him. She began to cry. Her ordeal was over.

He patted her on the shoulder.

"There, there now. You're safe with me. We'd better call the sheriff. I'm sure he and your parents are going to be very happy to hear that you are safe."

Charlie helped her to his shack. Megan had difficulty walking because of her tender feet. Once inside his cabin, he found a blanket to wrap around her. She sat in his old chair. Charlie dialed the sheriff.

"Sheriff Joe Wagner. This is Charlie Wright. Yes, I found a body, but this one is alive and well. She just swam up to my dock about 30 minutes ago. Her feet are very sore, but otherwise she is fine. Yes, you may talk to her."

Charlie handed Megan the phone.

"Yes, this is Megan Tyler. I'm all right. Please call my mom. Yes, I know who kidnapped me. They are Chad Harmon, Ted Horner, Cecil Dusenberg, Danny Walton, and Jake Burns. They are all at Doctor Walton's cabin."

There was a pause and silence.

"Yes, I know I am right. I went to school with all of them. Yes, I know they have fathers with big names . Actually, Ted and Jake tried to talk Chad and the others out of torturing me. They ran away. Chad Harmon took a couple of shots at them with a gun. I heard the pickup leave but I don't know where they are."

"Yes, they should still be there at Dr. Walton's cabin. Sheriff Joe, when you call my mother, have her bring some clothes for me. I have nothing on. I'm naked. The guys stripped me and cut my hair off. I have nothing to wear but this blanket the nice Mr. Wright gave me. Thank you, Sheriff."

Megan was relieved. Charlie asked her if she would like to lie down.

"I'm so tired, I could sleep on rocks," she answered.

Charlie took her to his bedroom. He pulled back the covers.

"I just washed everything yesterday. I've only slept here one night," he explained, "I'll see if I can find and old shirt of mine, you can wear. I'll be back in minute."

Charlie left the room. Megan dropped her blanket and crawled in. She was asleep before he returned. He tucked the covers around her shoulders and said, "Sleep, my little girl. Sleep as long as you want. Charlie will protect you."

Charlie laid his only dress shirt on the bed and returned back into the kitchen. He got his old shotgun down from the wall and loaded it. He wasn't taking any chances with this girl. He would protect her.

The sheriff barked out orders, "Jill , you go to the Tylers and tell them Megan is alive and at Charlie White's place. He is waiting for you and her parents. Take your EMT bag with you and check her out before she leaves Charlie's. Oh, and tell her mother to bring some clothes for her daughter. Apparently, she swam across the reservoir overnight naked.

Her captors stripped her before she got away."

It was six in the morning when Jill arrived at the Tylers'. Molly was in her pajamas and robe. She looked as if she had been through Hell, no make-up, hair not combed and bags under her eyes. She was in her pajamas only because Fred told her to try and relax. He was upstairs shaving, when Molly saw the deputy's car pull up. She was afraid to open the door when Jill arrived. She thought Jill was bringing bad news.

"Mrs. Tyler, I have news about your daughter," Jill announced.

"Yes," Molly said with an air of apprehension.

"Charlie Wright found your daughter. In fact, she found him. She is alive and is in his cabin on the south side of the lake. I'm to take you there. Megan told the sheriff she needed some clothes. Her kidnappers burned all the ones she had on. She swam across the lake to Charlie's. Charlie said she had some very sore feet. I'm an EMT and I'm going to check her out when we get there."

Molly grabbed Jill and hugged her. She called Fred and told him the good news. She couldn't stop crying for happiness.

"Fred, you wait here with the deputy while I change and get Megan some clothes. She's okay. Praise the Lord!"

Fred talked with Jill while they waited. "Does she know who kidnapped her?"

"Yes, the sheriff is on his way to arrest them right now. Your daughter swam across the lake during the night. It is more than three miles. She must be some kind of swimmer."

"She is," Fred said with a big smile.

Fred and Molly followed Jill to Charlie's cabin. He greeted them on the porch.

"She's sound asleep in my bed. She was very tired when she arrived here this morning. Just be quiet and don't scare her when you wake her up," Charlie explained like he was her father.

Molly, Jill, and Fred entered the room.

"Megan, Megan, wake up. It's me. Mom's here ," her mother whispered as she tapped Megan on the shoulder.

Megan rolled over and opened one eye.

"Mommy, mommy," she cried. She sat up and reached for her mother's open arms. She didn't care if the blanket fell to her waist . That was nothing after what she had been through. She hopped out of bed and hugged her dad. He hugged back. He put his hand on her bald head.

"It'll grow back, Daddy. It'll grow back."

He nodded. He was so glad to see her. Her mom tried to cover her bare body.

"Oh, Mom, "she said, "this is my daddy. I don't care. I'm safe in his arms . Aren't I, Daddy?"

"Yes, you are, my lovely daughter, but maybe you should let your mom put some clothes on you. Jill is an EMT. She will check you out before we go home. I'll leave while you get dressed. See you soon."

Fred exited the room and talked to Charlie. Molly and Jill checked Megan's feet and her vitals and helped her get dressed. When Megan came out of the bedroom, she limped over to Charlie and gave him a big hug and a kiss on his fuzzy cheek.

"Thank you, Charlie. Thank you for helping me. You can come over for a meal at anytime."

Charlie replied, "I never saw such a pretty girl and I never thought anyone could swim clear across this lake. God bless you, child."

Joe called Peg Palmer, "I think we have a break in the case. We found two young men who say they are part of a gang called the Wolf pack?" They came from the Walton cabin. Hurry! Let's all meet at my office before going out there. The missing girl is alive. She swam across the lake and is at a cabin on the opposite side. I talked to her on the phone and will notify her parents. Jill is going there as I speak. I sure they will overjoyed. The girl told me her captors are probably are still asleep. They had had quite a few beers. I'm sending a deputy to Titusville with the young men's parents One of the three left at the Walton cabin is armed. We will have to careful. Kids do stupid things when they are cornered."

Peg answered back, "I can be at the office in ten minutes. Can we have some backup out at the cabin?"

"Yes, I called everyone in. four deputies will be able to be there."

Back in Warrenville, Sheriff Joe lined up the deputies. He wanted three squad cars and four deputies. Peg arrived. They would drive in and surround the cabin. He had obtained a search warrant from Judge Smith.

Sheriff Joe and his deputies arrived at Dr. Walton's cabin around eight. The gate was locked. He cut the lock with bolt cutters. He didn't want to use the code the doctor had given him because it rang an alarm at the house.

They slowly drove up the long lane. The four men spread out around the building. Sheriff went to the door and knocked. No one came to the door. Peg turned the knob. It was unlocked. The pair walked in with their guns drawn.

Joe called out, "Is anyone here?"

They heard a shuffling of feet. A young man appeared at a door to the back rooms. He was in his underwear. When he saw the drawn guns and the officers, he put his hands in the air.

"Whaaaaat doooo you want?" he asked.

"Are you Cecil Dusenberg?" asked the sheriff.

"Yes."

"You are under arrest for kidnapping, torture, sexual harassment, underage drinking, and maybe murder. Do you know anything about this?"

"Yes, sir."

"Are there others here also?"

"Yes, sir." Cecil said, hanging his head. He knew it was over.

Joe grabbed Cecil and shoved him outside.

"Deputy, read him his rights. We're going in to fetch the others."

This time Peg hollered out, "Is anybody else here?"

Danny appeared, his hands held high. He also was undressed, but he came peacefully. He was shocked and totally embarrassed when he saw Peg standing there. Chad followed. He had a pistol in his hand.

Peg ordered, "Put the gun down, young man. Don't do anything stupid. We can fire twice as fast as you can."

Chad knew he was through. He laid the gun on the table and put his hands up. Joe led him outside.

"Can we get some clothes?" whined Danny.

"Yes, Peg will go with you, but be careful. She's a cop."

"Yes, sir, but can't a man come instead of her."

The sheriff smiled, "No, I think Lieutenant Palmer will do just find. I could have her strip search you if I wanted."

Peg snapped back at him with a smile, "I'd be happy to, Sheriff. Do I start with the big boy?"

Danny was mortified. He held onto his shorts tightly.

"Well, maybe not now. I think they are clean."

All three were standing on the porch in their underwear when Chad claimed he was innocent.

"No, you're not. You're the most guilty of all," stated Cecil. "Did you find Megan, Sheriff?"

"Yes, we did, She swam across the lake last night and was discovered by Charlie Wright. She is okay."

"And what about Ted and Jake?"

"They are both in the Titusville Hospital recovering from gunshot wounds. Do you know anything about that?"

"Yes, I believe I do." replied Danny.

Cecil broke down and cried. Chad scoffed at him. He cussed the deputies when they tried to handcuff him. He swung at them. They wrestled him to the ground and cuffed him.

The sheriff said, "Megan tells me you fellows have photos of her and the rest of the women you brought here. Is that right?"

"No," screamed Chad.

Danny spoke up. "Yes, we do. They're on a computer in my bedroom. Our costumes are under my bed in a big box. I'm sorry this happened, Sheriff. We didn't mean to have the others drown . It was Chad who started it. First, we just watched porn films, then Chad wanted more. We decided to try local girls. Chad would take girls to a remote spot and have them undress, then he took photos and videos of them. He'd threaten them with Facebook if they told. One time, we got Betty Purcell drunk and brought her out here.

We made her do awful things. Then, there was Sandi Young. We made her undress and serve us pizza naked. After that we drew on her body with markers. It just got worse and worse. He wanted more and more."

"Shut up! Danny, they have nothing on us, yet. Just let my Dad take care of us. He'll show these dumb cops." screamed Chad.

The wolf pack was loaded in the squad cars. When they got back to town, they could phone their parents. It was a great day for the Sheriff and the town of Warrenville, but a sad day for five young men and their families . It was obvious the parents of these young men were not in touch with what they were doing. Money had paid for the crimes to this point. The crimes their sons faced were now much more serious than sexual fantasies. The families of Cindy Connors, Shelly Williams and Vonda Jenkins now had closure. They knew no other young women would suffer the same fate as their daughters. Stacy and Amanda were no longer afraid to go outside their town. They along with Megan were the star witnesses for the state.

Miller's Falls

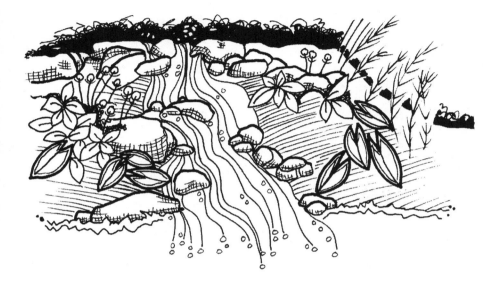

Janelle Fisher was fourteen and an athlete. She lived at the edge of a large tree plantation in northern Georgia with her mother, Donna, and father, Paul. She had a brother, Brad, who was ten years older and a sister, Danielle, eight year her senior. They were both married and had lives of their own.

Janelle had attended Jackson Middle School, but she would enter Bremerville High School in the fall. While in middle school, she tried out for chorus. Music was not on her radar, but at the urging of her mother she tried out for vocal chorus. She made the all-girl chorus, but not the elite a capella choir. The girls in all-girl were those who did not qualify for the a capella or show choir. She tolerated the chorus and its members for her mother.

She wasn't a tall girl, so basketball was not her forte. She went out for the team and made the squad, but rode the bench. She became discouraged and was about to drop the sport when the coach told her she admired her quickness. Coach encouraged Janelle to try out for track and cross-country running.

The running team was always short of athletes, so she was readily accepted. She loved the individual benefits of the sport. Soon she was the star cross-country runner at Jackson Middle school. The school was small by Georgia standards, only 300 students. She discovered her legs would carry her to the athletic heights she desired.

During a middle school meet, she caught the eye of the high school track coach. He encouraged her to try out for the high school team in August. He gave her pointers and a practice schedule. He told her he could see her at the varsity level as a freshman, if she ran most of the summer break. Janelle was excited, to say the least.

She ran right over to her mother in the stands and said, "Coach Harder wants me to try out for the cross-country team next fall. He gave me a practice schedule. Do you think I could do it, Mom?"

"Sure, but you'll have to practice almost every day. We could map out a trail to Miller's falls. I'll bet it is two miles to the falls. That'd be four miles round trip. We can ask your dad if the lumber company would allow you to use the trail. We wouldn't want to trespass."

Janelle turned to go back to the track when she saw Coach Harder heading her way. He stopped her and asked, "May I talk with your mother, Janelle?"

"Sure, she's sitting right over there," Janelle replied, pointing to her mother.

Janelle returned to the track as one of her events, the 400 meter, was about to start. Distance running was her specialty. While she waited, she watched the high school coach visit with her mother. Her mother was shaking her head with yeses and nos. Finally, they shook hands and the coach returned to watch the next event.

On the way home, Janelle's mother told her about her conversation with Coach Harder.

"He seems like a very nice man. He told me he thought you had great potential as a distance runner. He said in today's world, colleges are looking for good female athletes. He has several connections with major universities, and if you work hard, he thought there might be a scholarship available. He did realize it is a long way off, but time flies, and in three years, colleges start their recruiting. He also said he'd check on you during the summer."
"Great! I'll start practicing right away." Janelle squealed in delight.

Scholarships and colleges. Wow! she thought to herself.

Janelle was up early the next morning. She wanted to get her run in before school. She lived on a gravel road called the Old Tipton Road, which used to be the main road between Bremerville and Tipton. Twenty years ago, the state moved the highway about a mile to the west. It was paved and much better for the lumber trucks. Occasionally, a truck load of logs would travel the old road, because they were cutting trees with access to the gravel highway. Otherwise, the only traffic was local residents and service vehicles.

The road ran past several little square houses. They used to be the residences of the many workers at the lumber mill. Today, only five houses remained. Three were used by single employees and were in poor condition. In one of the remaining lived Jamal and his mother Rachel. They were allowed to live in the small building for free. Jamal's father was killed in an accident at the mill. Jamal himself had a handicap. His left arm was severed just below the elbow. When he was three, he put his hand into a sorghum mill and was pulled into the machine up to his elbow. His father pulled him free, but he lost his arm in the process. He was Janelle's friend and playmate for many years.

The home across the road from Jamal's house belonged to the Coffmans. They were a big family and very poor. Mr. Coffman worked in maintenance at the plant. The mother was always ill and could barely do housework and cook for her brood of four children. There were three girls and one boy in the family. The girls were all much younger than Janelle, but the boy, Bert, was in her class at school.

He was quite different from Jamal. He was big for his age. He was almost six feet tall and weighed over 200 pounds. He knew he was the biggest boy in the class and exploited his size. He bullied many of his peers. The only person who liked him was the football coach. His size made him a great candidate for a lineman and, at times, the one player who could punch the football into the end zone.

Both young men watched Janelle as she ran past their homes. Sometimes she would wave at Jamal, but not Bert. She didn't like the way Bert leered at her as she ran past.

School was dismissed before Memorial Day, but Janelle continued to run every morning. The red Georgia road dust sometimes covered her as she ran, especially when a log truck passed. A couple of times, she was run off the road because of the thick dust. She had several close calls, but it didn't deter her running.

One morning in late June, Janelle headed out. She passed Jamal's house, but he wasn't on the porch to wave. She thought, *He could be in town with his mother, or just doing some chores out back.*

As she approached Bert's house, she could see him walking out to the road.

"Hi, Janelle," he called to her.

"Good morning, Bert," she replied.

"Want to have a glass of iced tea?" he asked.

"No, thank you."

"Why? Ain't I good enough for you?"

Janelle slowed to a walk as she drew nearer. "I carry extra water in my backpack. Thanks anyway."

She was almost past when Bert reached out and grabbed her arm.

"I want to talk to you, Janelle."

"I don't want to talk to you because you are rude, crude, and smell bad. You hurt your sisters to get your way. You are not nice."

"How do you know if I hurt my sisters?"

"I see them in the cafeteria and they have bruises on their arms and legs. One time Missy had a black eye. She told me you hit her."

"It's a lie."

"Let go, Bert, you're hurting my arm."

Bert started pulling Janelle toward his yard. She struggled to free herself. He was strong and wouldn't let go. In desperation, she sank her teeth into his dirty arm. He screamed in pain and released his hold. Janelle scooted away.

Bert called after her, threatening, "I'll get you for this, Janelle Fisher. You'll wish you never knew me."

He gave her the bird as she disappeared around the corner. When Janelle reached the highway, she called her mother on her cellphone.

"Mom," she cried, "Bert Coffman attacked me this morning. I bit his arm to get away. I'm afraid to run back home."

"I can't come right away. Maybe your dad can take some time off. I'll call him."

Sure enough, Janelle's father arrived in ten minutes.

"What's this about Bert Coffman attacking you?"

"I was running by his house and he came out to the road and grabbed me by the arm. I tried to get away, but he wouldn't let go. So I bit him on the arm. He let go and I ran away. I was afraid to return the same way I came."

Paul answered, "I'll talk to Bert's father when I get home."

"Maybe you should quit running for a while."

"But, Dad, I have to practice if I want to make the team. What about the old timber road to Miller's Falls?"

"I don't know about that. It is company property and they don't want any liability problems. You may have to curtail your running until we can make it safer for you."

"Okay, but think about it, will you."

That night Janelle asked her father again if he would ask the company for permission to run the trail to Miller's Falls. Her father, Paul, worked as a forester for Acme Lumber and Pole company. The company's specialty was logs for poles and posts. The offal from their cutting was shipped to the nearby paper mill at Kilburn. His job was to oversee the harvesting, replanting, and growing of the trees on the company's land and several private plots the company managed.

The grove in which he and his family lived was young. It would be harvested in 15 years or more. The timber road beside their home ran all the way to Miller's Falls and beyond. It wound through the forest and ended behind the mill at Bremerville. For many years, it was used by teenagers going to the Falls for a swim in the lower pool formed by the water. The company didn't care as long as the young people picked up after themselves. In the early years, liability for accidents was not an issue.

Then one day a young man dove from the top of the falls and broke his neck. Now he was a paraplegic. The family sued and after a long, costly legal battle, the two parties agreed to a settlement. The next day, the road was closed. Janelle's father ordered several trees cut and laid across the road. This blocked all car and ATV traffic. No one was interested in walking the two miles to the falls. Soon the road was overgrown except for a narrow path for Paul's ATV. He kept his path open and smooth by dragging a small harrow behind his vehicle. It would be prefect for a cross-country runner.

The next day, Bert's father stopped Paul outside the gate to the plant.

"My son, Bert, told me your daughter bit him on the arm. She bit him so hard, I had to take him to the emergency room, and he had to have two stitches to close up the wound."

Paul looked at the accuser and replied, "Mike, my daughter told me Bert grabbed her as she ran by your house. She bit him to get away."

"I don't believe it."

"Janelle has the right to run any time on public roads. He should not attack her or try and stop her."

"Well, do you know what she's wearing? Those short shorts and flimsy top. She was trying to entice my son. She shouldn't be let out of your house," commented Mike, trying to change the subject.

"She is just wear typical running clothes like anyone else. It should be your son who should be confined. And Mike, how do you know what my daughter wears? Do you sit at home, too, and watch her? I think you should take another look at your accusations."

"I'm not saying anything, but you keep your daughter off the road or I'll call the cops." Mike threatened.

Paul rolled his eyes and walked away. Arguing with an irate father was useless.

That afternoon, Janelle's dad approached the forest supervisor with the request. He explained the situation. He told his boss he didn't want to cause any trouble with Mike Coffman. His boss approved the request with one stipulation: any accidents or injuries were not the company's liability. Janelle and her dad agreed. Janelle could begin practicing immediately, if both she and her father signed a no fault agreement.

It was cool and cloudy the first morning she started. Her mother, who also ran and was very athletic-looking, decided to run with her, just to learn about the path and its irregularities. The path was bordered by tall, 30-year-old trees for the first quarter mile, then the trees reduced in size to about six to seven feet due to a recent harvesting five years ago. These shorter trees continued for more than a mile, almost to the falls. The trees around the falls were still old growth due to the extreme difficulty of harvesting them. The terrain was just too steep and rocky.

The road followed the creek bed most of the way, with higher ridges on either side of the road. Halfway up the trail, the sun broke through the clouds. The air warmed quickly. It was a beautiful run with the contrast of tall pine, shorter younger pine, and old growth pine and its undergrowth. As they approached the falls, the trees formed an arch over the road and just as they were less than 200 feet from the falling water, the trees parted to let copious amounts of warm Georgia sunshine bask the pool area beneath the falls.

Janelle and her mother paused at the edge of the clearing. It was so pristine and quiet. The falls were pouring over the smooth rocks this morning, because of the recent rains in the area. The pool below rippled with little waves splashing upon the rocks.

"Isn't this beautiful," commented Donna.

"Yes, I remember coming here with you and Dad for a picnic. I wanted to go in the water, but we hadn't brought my swimsuit. You said it would be all right to go in my underpants. Dad said, 'Why get them all wet? There's nobody here and she's only six. She can swim with nothing on.' So I did. It was so much fun and I felt so free."

"Do you remember anything else?"

"I remember you and Daddy coming in, too. We all played and swam in the cool water with no clothes on. You told me not to watch Daddy get out of the water."

"Did you?"

"Mom, I won't lie. Yes, I did peek through my hands when Daddy crawled out on a slippery rock and fell back in. He looked funny with his head under water and his legs sticking out. You had to rescue him. He was so embarrassed because I saw him and his white pimply butt."

"Yes, that was sort of funny, and he skinned his leg in the tumble."

"You told him to cover his eyes when we got out, but he just sat there and grinned. He stared at you as you dried off. I think he loved watching you naked, and I think he still does. I caught you and him walking off to the timber one night when the moon was full. All you had on was a towel and he had on his under shorts. I heard you laughing a little later. I stayed awake until you returned. You were walking hand in hand and you both had nothing on."

"So you saw us. Well, I will tell my young daughter. Your mother and father love each other very much. Sometimes, on the spur of the moment, he has these silly fantasies. I play along with him and most times those fantasies are very fun. There is just something about walking naked with your spouse that makes love special. I hope someday you will be able to experience the same feeling. As for us doing it as a family, I don't think so now. That was a long time ago. You were a small child and now you are a grown-up girl. Be careful of men and boys, they will like to see you with nothing on, too. Only they won't be your daddy or mother. They may want to harm you. Just like Bert. He's big for his age and more mature. He may want to touch you and hold you. Beware of his advances," Donna warned.

"Now, let's sit down by the pool and cool our feet off before we return."

The pair found a rock close enough to dangle their feet in the water. They removed their shoes and socks and dipped their warm feet in the cool water. Donna slipped her backpack from her shoulders. It held some cookies and bottled water. They snacked and sipped some water. The sun was warm. Janelle closed her eyes and lay back on the rock. Her mother looked at her dozing daughter and pushed one of her socks into the water.

"Oh, shoot, Janelle, one of your socks just fell into the water," she with a giggle in her voice.

Janelle jerked up. "Now what will I do? I can't run without any socks on."

"I guess you will just have to go and retrieve it."
"But then I'll get my whole outfit wet," Janelle replied with disgust.

"Well, you could strip off our clothes and go in nude. Then you wouldn't get your precious running outfit wet."

"You mean I should go skinny dipping? Isn't that a little risky, or should I say risqué?"

"Why not? There's nobody here but you and me. I think I will take a dip, too."

"Okay, this will be fun. Boy, I never thought I'd go skinny dipping with my mother."

The pair helped each other out of their outfits. Since their backs were sweaty and wet, their tops were difficult to remove. Donna leapt in first. She screamed because of the chilly water, but soon was swimming and laughing.

"Come on in, the water's fine," she kidded her naked daughter.

Janelle took a short running jump and landed beside her mother. The water was shockingly cold below the surface. When she surfaced, she, too, let out scream. Her mother laughed and swam toward the bottom of the falls. She crawled out and walked in behind the falling water. Next she dove through the falling liquid. The weight of the water forced her deep into the pool. Donna was a good swimmer and she swam under water until she surfaced alongside Janelle.

Janelle scolded her. "Don't do that again. It's scary. I thought you might have drowned."

"I used to do that all the time, but I must admit it was later in the summer and the flow was much less."

After half an hour, Donna swam to the pile of clothes and said, "We better get out and head back home. I've got a two o'clock hair appointment. Since we have no towels, we'll have to dry in the sun. Such a pity."

After Janelle and her mother lay in the sun for a few minutes, they dressed and slowly jogged down the forest road home. The road was not only safe, but beautiful. The trees and the birds made the run a joy. Janelle began running every day but Sunday. Earlier in the morning was better because the dew made the leaves and grass sparkle and the air seemed so fresh.

One day, Donna came home with a proposal for Janelle.

"I have client in the shop who needs a babysitter Friday, Saturday, and Sunday. She has two little girls four and six. I suggested you might be interested. You could still run the other four days. The good part is, I could drive you there Thursday evening and they would bring you home on Sunday."

"You mean I would sleep at their house?"

"Sleep, bathe, cook, play, and protect the little darlings. She told me she would pay $150 per weekend."

"How long will the job last?'

"Until August fifteenth, then her job goes back to five days during the week."

"Sounds almost too good to be true. Tell her yes, I'll try it."

Janelle soon found that taking care of two little ones by herself was tiring. When she got home on Sunday evening, it was usually late. She was too tired to run the next morning, so she settled for running three days a week. It was getting warmer in Georgia anyway, so three days were plenty.

The Fourth of July weekend was a three-day affair this year. The family Janelle was sitting for, went out of town, so she could go with her family to the big company picnic. It was a large affair and many of Janelle's friends were there. Between the many games being played, Janelle found Jamal at the drink stand.

"Hi, Janelle, haven't seen you running by my house lately. Did you give it up?" asked Jamal.

"No, I just run three days a week. I have a babysitting job on the weekends. I've changed my route, too. Now I run the old timber road to Miller's Falls. It is safer, with no dust, and Bert can't bother me."

"Bert? What did he do?"

"Didn't you hear about Bert and me? He grabbed me as I ran by his house. He wouldn't let me free, so I bit him. I guess I bit him good because his father talked to my dad and said he had to have three stitches in his arm."

"Wow! I sure did miss that one. I've got a babysitting job, too. I sit two boys all week and have my weekends off. No wonder we don't see each other."

Janelle and Jamal chatted a while, not noticing Bert Coffman standing close by. He was listening very intently. He grinned to himself. Janelle would soon know who he was and she would not scorn him anymore.

The following weeks, Janelle continued her routine of Tuesday, Wednesday and Thursday trekking up to Miller's Falls and back. She would stop at the falls for a break, take her shoes and socks off, and dip her feet in the cool water. She loved listening to the birds singing in the trees and tried to identify which song fit which bird. Only once she did think of taking a dip in the cool pool.

This day was no different. It was a warm mid-July day. Janelle was sweating profusely as she approached Miller's Falls. The water looked inviting. The falls, which was actually a series of rapids, was flowing between the ridges in the cliff. This time of year, the creek ran full and cool. It wasn't fed by runoff, but by cool mountain springs further up the mountain.

Janelle took off her shoes and socks and dangled her feet in the water. She loved this little personal paradise. Today she was alone, or thought she was alone. She had the funny feeling she was being watched. She scanned the dense foliage around the pool to see if there was any sign of an intruder. She couldn't see or hear anything, only the babbling falls and a few birds. In the distance, a woodpecker rattled the silence with his rat-a-tat-tat.

She cut her stay short. As she was cruising home along the logger's road in the area where the trees were young, she thought she spied a figure ducking from tree to tree. The figure was on the ridge above her road. She stopped a couple of times to make sure she wasn't seeing things, but each time she stopped, whatever it was hid quickly. Should she tell her mother?

That evening at the supper table, Janelle told her parents about her intruder. They tried to figure out what she saw. Donna decided she would run with Janelle on Thursday. Of course, nothing happened. The following Tuesday, Janelle spotted the same figure, but this time she thought she recognized who it was. She thought it was Bert. She'd fix him when got home. *I'll call his house and if he isn't there, I'll know it was him.*

As soon as she got home, she opened the phone book and found Coffman's number. She dialed it.

"Hello, Coffmans, this is Missy."

"Missy, this Janelle Fisher. Is Bert home?"

There was a pause and some whispering, followed by Missy saying, "Ouch!"

"No, he's not here. He is at his uncle Henry's baling hay and chopping peanuts. He'll be gone till school starts. Do you want me to have him call you?"

"Oh no, I just wanted to see if he was home. I thought I saw him on the road. It wasn't important. Thanks anyway."

Janelle hung up the phone. If Bert is at his uncle's, then it couldn't have been him on the ridge. Maybe it was just a coincidence. She could be at peace now she knew he wasn't around.

At the Coffman house, it wasn't so pleasant.

Missy was screaming, "Bert, let go of my arm. You're hurting me. I'll tell Dad when he gets home."

"Oh no you won't, cause I've got your pet kitten and I'll wring his neck if you say anything," Bert answered with a sneer. "Thanks for lying to Janelle. Now you can have your mangy kitten back."

The next week was hot and humid in Georgia, really hot and humid. The temperature was in the nineties and humidity about the same. Janelle left home earlier than normal. She first had to run to the mailbox and mail some letters for her mom. She looked down the road at the Coffman house. Out front, next to the road, Missy stood holding something that looked like a kitten. She was looking across the road. Janelle didn't think much of it at the time.

She returned to the house and picked up her water bottles and snacks. It would be warm early. The dew was still on the leaves of the honeysuckle. The young pines smelled wonderful in the morning. She wore her new green and gold running outfit. They were the colors of Bremerville High School. Her tank top was green with a broad gold stripe running diagonally across her chest. Her shorts were green with reflective gold stripes on each side. She wanted gold shoes, but her mother balked at the extra expense.

Her black backpack swung on her back. The water bottles inside cooled her back as she ran. She quickened her pace as she ran through the young trees because there was little shade there. Even with her hurried pace, she was very warm when she reached the pool below the falls. She sat on the only shaded rock near the pool, took off her shoe and socks, and dipped her hot feet into the cool water. She splashed the water with her toes. It was so comforting to know Bert was nowhere around. She was all alone at her little piece of paradise. She slid from her rock and stepped into the cool water. She stood there knee deep in the cool liquid. The hot sun beat down on her and just standing in the water was not doing the job.

Why don't I take off my shorts and wade deeper? There's nobody here, she told herself.

She stepped back on shore and slipped her shorts down. She stared at the water for a bit more.

Why not go all the way? Mom and I did just a few days ago.

She stripped off her tank top and struggled to pull her bra over her head because she was so sweaty. She laid her clothes on a rock, her shorts and sport underpants on the bottom, her tank top next, and bra on top. She set her shoes and socks beside her backpack.

Once she was naked, the slight breeze was cooling against her skin. She didn't waste any time and dove into the water. It felt so good. She swam to the falls, which were now just a trickle coming over the edge. She let the water trickle over her head, then she flipped over and floated slowly back to the opposite shore. She closed her eyes as she floated. Her quiet float was broken by a voice laughing.

"Well, well, well, looky who we have here. Little Miss Wonderful Runner. I wonder if these are her clothes."

Janelle jerked to a standing position. Her feet barely touched the rocky bottom. She shaded her eyes and saw Bert Coffman standing with her clothes in his hand.
"Bert Coffman, you put my clothes back and get away!" she screamed.

"Not on your sweet bippy, sweetheart. It looks like I have the upper hand. I have your clothes and you are stuck in the water with nothing on. I say you come and get them. I always wanted to see you naked. You know, nude, as in one of those men's magazines. I'll bet you're really cute."

"No, never."

Bert started to walk away with her clothes in his hands. He grinned and said, "I guess you'll have to walk home naked and explain to your mother how come your clothes made it home before you did."

"Bert, you big bully, quit picking on poor defenseless little girls." Janelle tried her whimpering helpless little girl mode.

"Sorry, Miss Fisher, it won't work. I have you at quite a disadvantage. You do as I say or you walk home naked as a jaybird. It's your decision."

Janelle kept treading water and pondering what to do. She really didn't want to get out of the pool with Bert, the bully, watching her every move. Worst of all, she would be naked. She swam closer to shore and Bert. She knelt down in the shallower water in front of Bert. She gazed up at him and found him smiling as he looked down at her. The water was very clear.

"I see your tits, Janelle. They look nice under water," commented Bert with a grin.

Janelle crossed her arms across her chest. "You pig!"

"Oh, come on, Miss Janelle Fisher, name-calling will get you nowhere."

Janelle knew she was in trouble. Maybe if she gave him what wanted to see, he'd be satisfied.

"Okay, Bert, if I come out will you give me my clothes back?"

"Yeah, maybe, but I'm going to lay them by the road."

"By the road? Why not right here on this rock?"

"Cause I want to see you naked and if I put them on the rock you'll grab them and go back into the pool. You see I'm not so dumb after all."

"Okay."

Bert lay the green outfit in a pile near the roadbed. He hurried back to watch Janelle step out of the water. Janelle cautiously felt her way to shore. Getting to shore was tricky since the shoreline was not sandy, but made of big granite rocks a billion years old. She placed both hands on the nearest stone to balance herself. She didn't realize Bert stood just above her with a small rope formed into a noose. As she brought her head up, the noose fell over her head. Instantly, she grabbed the rope. Bert pulled the noose tighter.

"Stop, Bert, you're choking me!"

"Yeah, I know. Do what I say and I won't pull it any tighter. Follow me."

"But my clothes?"

"Oh, yes, your duds. Well, here's what I think of them."

Bert picked up her outfit and tossed it into a nearby honeysuckle bush. All Janelle could do was watch. She kept one hand on the rope and tried to cover herself with her free hand. Bert just chuckled at her attempt. He pulled the rope tighter. Janelle was forced to use both hands to keep the rope from choking her. This is just what Bert wanted, total control.

"Follow me. We're going into the trees and teach you a lesson of respect."

Janelle followed behind with both hands protecting her neck. The sharp stones on the road cut her feet and when they entered the forest, the carpet of pine needles was laced with sharp pine cones and twigs. Bert began looking for a special tree.

He lost his footing and stumbled, letting go of the rope momentarily. Janelle ducked and slipped the rope from her neck. She didn't hesitate but took off running further into the forest. Bert swore and started after his prey.

Janelle ran in territory where she hadn't been before. She didn't care, as long as it was away from Bert. She knew she could outrun him. She heard him puffing after her. She was extending the distance between them until she ran right into a six-foot-high fence. She hit the fence with such force that she tripped the trigger on the swinging spring-loaded gate. She was trapped. She tried climbing the wire fencing, but the wire cut her feet. She began running around the edge of the enclosure like a trapped animal.

Bert stopped outside and laughed. "I guess my little fox trapped herself."

Janelle cried out, "What is this?"

"This, my dear nude Janelle, is a feral hog trap. You're lucky for you there aren't any hogs in there with you. Now come over here by the gate and give me your hands."

Janelle had no choice. She meekly walked to the gate and held her hands out in front of her. Bert tied her hands together, then unlatched the gate. He scanned her body up and down.

"Do you enjoy what you see?" Janelle snarled back at him.

"Very much so, you have such nice tits. They are so firm and round. They're not like my mother's. They sag down."

"When do you see your mother's breasts? Do you watch her dress?"

"No, I just see her now and then. Sometimes her back hurts from her beatings and she takes off her bra and when she bends over I can see her boobs."

"What beatings?"

"Oh, my dad beats her when she is bad, just like I'm going to do to you right now."

He led his captive back toward the pond. They were in sight of the road when they stopped. He threw the rope over a low branch and pulled Janelle's arms up above her head. Janelle began to shake.

"What are you going to do to me?" she stammered.

"I am going to teach you a lesson about respect. Let's see, you called me a bully, five strikes, you called me a pig, ten strikes, you said I smelled, six strikes, and maybe five more for good measure. Let's see, 5 plus 10 plus 6 plus 5 equals 26."

"Twenty-six strikes? What are strikes?"

"You'll find out."

Bert moved close to Janelle. He slowly moved his hand down her back to her hips.

"It's a shame I have to ruin such a beautiful back. You should see my mother's." Bert said with a little remorse in his voice, "Open your mouth so I can stuff my hankie in it. I hate hearing women scream."

Janelle shook her head no.

"No!" Bert repeated, sounding surprised, "I say yes, and I know how to make you open your mouth. You'll do what I want you do to Miss Janelle Fisher."

Bert reached down and grabbed her breast, then he twisted her nipple with his thumb and forefinger.

"Ow!" screamed Janelle.

When she opened her mouth, he stuffed the filthy hankie in. He turned and left. Janelle hung there awaiting her fate. Bert returned swinging a willow switch in the air.

"I'm back," he chortled, "and here is your answer to what a strike is."

He laid one lash across her bare back. It left a bright red mark. Janelle jumped from the pain.

"One strike!" Bert started to count. "Twenty-five to go."

Janelle's eyes bugged out. The pain was ferocious. She couldn't scream. All she could do was jump and wiggle. Bert laughed. He struck again and again. The welts built up. At fifteen swats, her legs gave out. She hung by the rope.

"Get up! You bitch," snarled Bert as he struck the back of her legs. Janelle struggled to stand. She had eleven to go. Her captor started to ease up, or it seemed so. Janelle was so numb the last ones seemed lighter.

"Twenty-six!" called Bert. "Done."

He loosened the rope from the tree and Janelle collapsed on the ground. She pulled her legs up to her chest. Her hands were still tied together, but she could pull the filthy rag from her mouth. She sobbed. Her body was on fire.

Bert ordered, "Get up. I know I can't let you go back looking like this. You're going back in the pool to wash off the blood."

He reached down and grabbed the rope. He pulled her to her feet and headed for the pool. Janelle stumbled along. Her feet were sore from running in the rocky forest floor. She gave up on escaping; just surviving was the job of the day. Bert mumbled something.

"What did you say?" asked Janelle.

"I said you're going to the pool to wash up. Maybe I'll tie a big rock to your feet and let you sink to the bottom. It will be days before they find you and I'll run away from home. The cops won't pin your death on me. You know I'm supposed to be at my uncle's. If I turn you loose, you'll squeal on me."

Janelle pleaded, "No, no, Bert. I promise I won't tell. I'll say it was a hiker who caught me and beat me. I'll even walk home naked if you'd like."

"No, I think drowning would be best."

"Please, Bert, no. Here, touch my breasts. Kiss them if you want. I'll kiss you if you want. Do anything you want, just don't drown me."

Bert thought a minute. His eyes twinkled. He gave her a mischievous smile. "I know. I'll take my clothes off and you must suck my dick. Then we will go swimming together. After that, I get to touch you anywhere I want, even between your legs. Agreed?"

Janelle sighed and began to cry. She nodded her head.

The pair were about twenty feet from the clearing and passing a large Southern pine when from behind the trunk came the blur of a large stick. It hit Bert in the stomach. Bert doubled over in pain. He let go of Janelle's arm.

"Run, Janelle, run!" called a voice.

Janelle looked up and saw Jamal. He was swinging his arm at Bert's head. The stub knocked Bert to the ground. Bert rolled down the slight grade to get away and recover. He stood and dove for Jamal. He was furious. He lunged forward. Jamal countered by stepping lightly aside. Bert flew by, ramming his shoulder into a tree. He clutched his shoulder and turned to face Jamal.

"You, you, black nigger!" Bert screamed.

Janelle crawled across the path and hid under the honeysuckle bush. With her hands tied together, she scooped up the shorts and top that Bert had thrown there. From her hiding place, she watched the battle unfold. It was a David and Goliath fight, with David having only one hand. It was unfair. She worried what would happen to her and Jamal if he lost.

Bert and Jamal sparred for a couple of times, neither one gaining any advantage. Jamal had to continue to retreat from Bert's vicious advances. He stumbled backward. Bert was on him in a flash. Jamal rolled to his left, escaping the bigger boy's weight. Bert tried again, knowing if he could pin Jamal, it would be over. He could pound on Jamal until he submitted.
Jamal rolled again, and this time, his hand discovered the willow whip Bert had used on Janelle. He grabbed the whip and jumped up. Bert was still on his knees. Jamal caught him across the face with the whip. Bert howled and covered his face. Jamal attacked the big boy's middle. Bert rolled over on the ground. Jamal continued to beat his back until Bert cried, "I give!"

Jamal stopped. He stared at the trembling hulk of Bert's body.

"Get up and get out of here. If you ever lay one finger on Janelle Fisher again, I will kill you."

Bert struggled to his feet. Pine needles covered his T-shirt and his bare back. His shorts had slipped down in the fight and his butt crack showed. It too was stuffed with pine needles. He started to walk away, then stopped to say something. Jamal struck him again.

"Keep going, Bert."

Bert headed for the younger trees and the path home. He stopped once to brush the needles off. Jamal started after him with the switch. Bert quickly disappeared into the trees. Jamal watched him go. He got a big smile on his face. He had just beaten Bert, who was twice his size and had both hands. He felt pretty good until he heard a moan come from behind him. He had almost forgotten why he was there.

He peeked under the honeysuckle and called softly, "Janelle, are you there? Are you okay?"

Janelle crawled from beneath bush and looked up at Jamal.

"Is he gone?" she asked.

"Yes. Here, let me help you up."

Janelle slowly got to her feet and looked around, still worried about Bert. It looked safe. She wanted to hug and kiss Jamal.

"Oh, Jamal, I thought I was going to die, but you saved me. I want to hug you, but my hands are still tied. Can you help me untie this rope?"

Jamal tried with his one hand to squeeze the rope backwards through the knot. His fingers just wouldn't push it through and he had no other hand to hold the rope. He studied the knot and the rope again, trying not stare at Janelle. She was making no effort to hide her body. Even though she was bleeding on her back, she still was a very good-looking girl.
"I've got an idea," he told her.

He went over to the pond and picked up a small stone. He stepped back a couple of feet and threw the smaller stone against a boulder. It split, leaving a jagged edge. He hurried back to Janelle.

"I'll put this rock between my knees. You rub the rope over the jagged edge. I hope it will cut the rope."

He sat on a stump and stuck the fractured rock between his knees. Janelle took positon in front of him and placed the rope on the rock edge. She rubbed the rope back and forth. The rope started to fray.

"It's working, it's working," Janelle said excitedly. She began to rub the stone faster. Jamal was trying to avoid looking at Janelle, but her breasts and tummy attracted his eyes. He couldn't help but stare. Janelle looked at his eyes only once. She gave him a slight smile.

Jamal warned, "Watch it. Don't cut yourself. We have enough problems."

It took several minutes for the last stubborn stand to break. The rope fell away. Janelle rubbed her swollen hands. She had rope burns on her wrists. She shook her arms to revive the circulation. Jamal stood and threw the stone back toward the pool.

Janelle gazed at Jamal and said, "You're my hero. Thank you, thank you, thank you."

She jumped upon the stump next to the one he was sitting on and pulled him to her. She planted a big kiss and hugged him.

Jamal tried to be calm. He had never had a girl kiss him before, especially a naked one. He wanted to hold her, but her back was so sore. He just ran his hand down her side and held her hip. Janelle was shaking. At this time, modesty was not in play. She was just fine being held by someone. She let go when Jamal's hand touched her hip. She realized she was without any clothes and stepped from the stump saying, "Jamal, look at me. No, no, don't look at me."

But he did anyway and he liked what he saw. Janelle was athletic and thin. Her legs were firm and her tummy flat. Her junior-miss-sized breasts were lovely on her rib cage. Now her nipples perked out. He had never seen a woman in the nude except in some discarded men's magazines. Here he was with a neighbor friend standing stark naked in front of him and hugging him, and the sight wasn't cut off by some camera tricks. Her body was naked all the way from her head to her toes.
Janelle quickly turned away. Now Jamal saw her back was crisscrossed with ugly red welts. Her legs were swollen and almost bleeding. There were places on her back where blood had already scabbed over. Her wrists were bloody from the rope cutting them when she twisted and turned while hanging from the tree limb. Now he felt ashamed for looking at her.

Janelle sensed his embarrassment. "I'm a mess, aren't I? Jamal, don't feel embarrassed. I'm not. I'm just glad to be alive, naked or not. Right now, think of me as someone who needs help, and she looks like any other girl in the shower."

"But I've never seen any girls in the shower," Jamal blurted.

"I suppose not. Well, now you won't have to ever look. You've seen me. Now help me put on my shorts. I don't know what I will do for a top. I certainly can't wear my bra over these welts."

Jamal helped her step into her shorts and pulled them gingerly over her hips. He gazed at her upper body, then took off his sleeveless shirt, ran to the pool, dipped it in the cool water, wrung it out, and returned.

"Here, this will cover you and maybe soothe those cuts."

"Thank you, you're a peach."

Janelle slipped the shirt on. It was so long it almost went to her knees. She fumbled with the buttons. They were difficult since they were opposite of women's clothing and her fingers were swollen from being tied so tightly. The more she tried, the more the buttons refused to slip into the hole.

"Here, let me help," said Jamal.

He turned her to face him and began to button each button.

"Jamal, you're embarrassed again, aren't you? Your face doesn't show it, but I can tell by your eyes and the expression on your face. Tell you what. Let's leave the shirt unbuttoned until we get closer to home, then maybe my fingers will be better and I can do it myself."

Jamal smiled and said, "That is our next problem. How are we getting you home?"

"Let me try my shoes and maybe I can walk some. That stick really punctured my foot. While you're finding my shoes, maybe ol' Bert left us some water in my backpack. You've got to be thirsty."
Jamal hurried and found Janelle's shoes and discovered Bert had forgotten all about the backpack. The water was warm, but it was wet. Janelle struggled with her shoes. She tried walking, but the puncture wound on her foot hurt too badly.

"Maybe if I lean on your shoulder," she told Jamal.

Jamal put his good arm around her waist to steady her. He tried not to notice her breasts peeking out from the open shirt, but there they were. What should he do? He tried to pull the bottom closed, but that didn't work. Janelle could see his efforts were futile and the shirt was rubbing her back raw again.

"Let me see your foot. Sit here and let me look."

Janelle sat on the stump while Jamal removed her shoe.

"My, my, this is nasty. The stick must have gone in half an inch. There may be some wood still in there. Let me carry you to the water and let me wash it."

He picked her up and carried her to the edge of the pool. He took off his shoes and waded into the shallow water. He washed her injured foot. She winced as he massaged the reddened skin around the wound.

"I think it is the best I can do. Maybe I should carry you?" he suggested.

"How would you do that?"

"On my back. I carry my nephews around all the time."

"But I'm much heavier," she protested.

"Not by much. Let's try. If I have to rest halfway down, I will. Here, stand on this old stump. Put each leg around my waist and your arms around my neck."

Janelle listened to the plan. Next she noticed his sweaty back. This might work if he had his back covered. She slipped her arms from his shirt and said, "Here, you need this more than I do. Hand me my top. I think if I wear it without my bra, I'll be able to go. You can stuff my bra in your pocket."

Jamal helped with her top. He gently pulled it over her tender back.

The welts were becoming more red and prominent. The sweat from her fraying of the rope made the wounds sting. Beads of sweat dripped from her chin down her chest. She wiped her forehead with the tail of her top. The thin fabric became drenched and her nipples strained against her top. Jamal couldn't help but stare. She noticed him staring.
She smiled and turned sideways, saying, "Pretty sexy, huh."

Jamal didn't say anything; he just grinned a big toothy grin. She stepped up on the stump. Jamal backed up to her. She sort of leapt upon his back. He grabbed her legs and said, "Let's go!"

The pair started down the long two-mile path. Now the sun was very warm. Jamal stopped in the shade about half way.

"I need a break."

"Sure."

The two sat in the shade. Jamal drank the last of the water. Janelle sat next to the tree and folded her arms across her chest. She looked at Jamal and started laughing.

"What's so funny?" he asked.

"Us."

"Us? Why us?"

"Because here we sit, a black boy and half-naked white girl. If this would have occurred 100 years ago, you'd been swinging from a tree by your neck and I would be banished from the town. I'd be called a whore or harlot."

"Yeah, but, at least you wouldn't be dead."

They laughed and kidded for another ten minutes. They were like siblings.

Jamal announced, "Well, Miss Calendar Girl, we best be going."

"Calendar girl? Which month am I? June? July? I know, February, and I'm little cupid with no clothes on."

She struck a pose as if she were shooting an arrow. Jamal smiled at her antics. She tried to turn and moon him, but the welts on her back awoke and started complaining.

"Ow, ow ow." she cried. "You are right, let's get going. One more question."

"Shoot."

"How come you were at the falls? Aren't you babysitting anymore?"
"First, my aunt and uncle and family are on a vacation. Second, I saw Bert leave early this morning, heading up the shortcut path to the falls. Third, when I went to get our mail, Missy was by their mailbox, crying and holding a kitten. I walked across the road to see if I could help. She told me Bert had just killed her kitten. I asked, where he was now? She told me he was going to get even with that smartass Janelle Fisher. When she told him she'd tell their mother, he grabbed her kitten and strangled it. That's when I followed him up the mountain. Of course, I

was a bit late. He already had you beaten and bruised. I arrived right as he let you down."

"Oh, and not a minute too late. Another five minutes and I would have been fish bait. I thought Bert was at his uncle's. He's been spying on me ever since we had our little skirmish on the road. He must have waiting to for me to go swimming because nothing happened until I was in the water. According to you, he was going to get me clothed or naked. I just deprived him the joy of undressing me."

She climbed aboard his back again and off they trotted.

* *   **   **   **   **   **   **

It was two o'clock. Rachel called Donna and wondered if she had seen Jamal or Janelle. Donna replied, "No."

Rachel answered, "The sheriff is here. He wants talk with Jamal. Bert's father claims Jamal beat up his son."
"Oh my goodness. I'll try and call her."

Donna tried repeatedly to reach Janelle, but no answer.

She recalled Rachel and said, "I can't raise her. Something dreadful has happened. I'll be home in fifteen minutes."

When Donna reached home, two squad cars were waiting along with Rachel.

"I called Paul on my way over. He will be here soon."

One of the deputies walked over to the two women and asked, "Do you think there may be some foul play? I talked with the young man who claims he was assaulted, but I found his story to be inconsistent. I think something happened he is not telling me."

Donna answered, "Come with me. I know the way to the falls by way of the old logger's road. It is the one she runs every day."

"You lead the way, Mrs. Fisher. Mrs. Simpson, you and the others stay here in case the lost pair show up."

Donna and the deputy started up the logger's road, which now was just an over-grown path. About a third of a mile ahead of them, Jamal and Janelle were trotting down the path. Jamal was sweating profusely. He slowed his pace, then he stumbled.

Janelle asked, "Are you all right?"

"I don't know. I feel dizzy. Maybe we should rest."

He took two more steps and collapsed, throwing Janelle over his head. She landed on her side in the dirt. She recovered and crawled back to Jamal. He was unresponsive. His eyes were rolling back in his head. He was wringing wet with perspiration.

"Jamal. Jamal. Don't leave me. You're having a heat stroke. Listen to me we have to get you in the shade."

He didn't answer. Janelle's adrenaline started pumping. Her aches and pains were nullified. She grabbed his arms and pulled him to the nearest shade. She started to panic. She didn't want to leave him. She could barely walk. Then she realized she was only a few blocks from her house.

Maybe someone is home, she thought to herself.

She started to holler, "Help, help, please someone help!"

Just around the curve, her mother heard a cry.

"Is that someone crying for help?" she asked the deputy.

He shook his head as if he hadn't heard anything.

"There it is again. It's my daughter. Hurry."

Donna took off running with the officer trailing behind. As she rounded the bend in the path, she spotted Janelle hobbling toward her. They both saw each other at the same time. Janelle stopped. Donna rushed forward.

"What happened to you, Honey? Where are your shoes? Do you know where Jamal is? The sheriff is on his way. He wants to talk to Jamal." Janelle gave her a shocked look. "The sheriff wants to talk to Jamal. What for? He saved me from Bert Coffman. Right now he's lying under a tree just a few feet from here. He had a heat stroke from carrying me. He needs help now!"

Donna and the officer hurried ahead. Janelle hobbled behind. They found Jamal's limp body under the tree. Donna bent down and felt his pulse.

"He's still alive, but we need water and help, quickly."

The deputy called on his radio. "This is Deputy Horner. We found the lost girl and boy. The boy is in bad shape from what I'd call a heat stroke. We need immediate help. Send for an ambulance."

The answer came back. "Mr. Fisher is here. He will bring water and the boy's mother on an UTV. We'll send an EMT up as soon as they get here."

Janelle finally limped back to Jamal's tree. Her mother asked again, "What happened?"

"It was awful, Mom. I went for a dip in the pool and Bert Coffman caught me. He grabbed my clothes and taunted me. He made me get out naked, as I was climbing out I lost my balance. He slipped a rope around my neck. When he stumbled, I got away for a short bit. I didn't know there are feral hog traps in the woods. I got caught in one. Bert tied my hands and led me to a tree. He threw the rope over a branch and pulled my arms over my head. Mom, I was naked! He went for a willow switch and whipped me. See?" Janelle turned around and lifted her top to show the welts.

"Holy cow! exclaimed Deputy Horner. "You just sit down here, Miss. We'll get you some help."

"That's not all. Bert whipped me twenty-six times. I know; he counted. He told me when he was finished he couldn't let me go, so he was going to throw me into the pool with a rock tied to my feet. That's when Jamal surprised him and hit him with a stick. I ran and hid under a honeysuckle bush while they fought. Jamal finally found the whip Bert was using and beat Bert with his own weapon. Bert gave in and Jamal told him to get. Jamal helped me get dressed and cleaned my foot. I still couldn't walk, so he carried me. It is Bert Coffman who should be under arrest, not Jamal!"

There was a roar of an UTV. Paul and Rachel hopped out. Rachel ran to her son. She knelt and cried, "Jamal, don't leave me, please."

Jamal weakly opened one eye. He smiled at his mother. She kissed his cheek. They waited for the EMTs. Soon they came roaring up the path. They treated Jamal first. His body temperature was 104 degrees. Instantly, they poured water on him. One wet a sheet and laid it over him. The next UTV arrived with a stretcher. They placed Jamal on the back of the vehicle. One EMT rode on the tailgate holding a bottle of saline solution. Rachel hopped in on one side and Deputy Horner drove on the return to the Fisher home.

The attention now focused on Janelle. It was just Janelle, her parents, and a female EMT, Cara.

Cara asked, "Your name is Janelle?"

"Yes."

"Okay, Janelle, with your mother's permission, let's take a look at your backside."

Her mother nodded affirmative.

Cara pulled Janelle's top up to her neck. Janelle raised her arms and her mother slipped the top off. Next she lowered Janelle's shorts to her ankles. Janelle stood there patiently with nothing on. Her dad didn't know what to do. She was his daughter, but now she was a young woman. Janelle sensed his feelings. She said, "It's all right, Dad. I'm still your little girl."

Cara probed and pinched her welts as gently as she could. She looked at Donna and said, "I think the cuts are shallow, but there might be debris I can't see. Your daughter should go to the emergency room to be sure. I believe she can ride in your car and not require an ambulance."

She turned to Janelle and said, "Do you think you will be able to ride in the UTV if we take it slow?"

"We can do it, can't we, Dad?" Janelle answered.

Donna helped her daughter dress. Janelle and her mother rode on the tailgate. Janelle leaned on her mother's shoulder. She was exhausted, but this part of her treacherous day was over.

It was after five when Donna and Janelle reached the ER. She was ushered into the small examining room. A doctor and nurse popped in between the curtains.

"Mom, will you help your daughter undress and into a gown?"

"Sure."
"Just leave the back untied since that is where the injury is. We'll be back in two minutes."

Janelle quipped, "Here I go again. Getting naked for the fifth time today. I might as well become a nudist."

The pair exited and could be heard next door.

"Mrs. Simpson, your son is out of danger. His body temperature is back to normal. Except for a few bruises, he should be able to go home later this evening."

"Oh, thank you, Doctor. I was so afraid I had lost him."

The doctor and nurse returned to Janelle. They examined her back. The doctor ordered her back to be cleaned and each open cut searched for foreign material. He left and let the nurse finish the job. She washed and picked off the scabs. As she was working, Rachel opened the curtain.

"How is Janelle doing?" she asked.

Just as she asked, the nurse probed a deep cut on Janelle's fanny. She got some tweezers and dug into the cut. Janelle winched as the nurse extracted a half inch long splinter. She held it for all to see.

"Good thing we got this piece of lumber out of your hiney or you'd be back here in a couple of days with a real sore one. Now next I'm going to flush your back with an antiseptic. Mom, you hold her hand because this is going to burn for a bit."

The nurse swabbed the liquid on her sore back. Janelle didn't say a word, but she about crushed her mother's hand and tears rolled down her face. Rachel watched and shed some tears also.

When the burning stopped, Donna asked, "How is Jamal doing?"

"He's stable now. The doctor said he could go home this evening."

Rachel stepped over to Janelle's bed and handed her bra to her. She winked at Donna and said, "Jamal said he saw a lot of your daughter this morning. I found Janelle's bra in his pocket."

Janelle spoke quickly. "He was a gentleman all the time and I must say quite embarrassed."

The trio snickered.
The next day, Mike Coffman confronted Paul Fisher at the gate of the mill.

"I heard you filed charges against my son," Mike inquired.

"You heard right," was the answer.

"Well, last night my son admitted he abused your daughter and the black boy was just defending her. I'll drop the charges if you will."

"I'm afraid you're going to be disappointed, Mike. Your son beat Janelle badly. She also told me he threatened to drown her just to cover up his abuse. I'm going to continue with my charges. Your son needs help. Maybe the courts will help him, because you're certainly not."

Mike's face turned red. "But Bert said your daughter was swimming naked in the pool and she enticed him."

"Now, Mike, she told me she was swimming nude, but I doubt she was enticing Bert to beat her. He was just trying to scare her. I'll bet if the authorities look around the falls some more, they will find he has been spying on her for a long time. He's stalking her, among other crimes. Another thing. I don't know where in that Holy Bible of yours it says you can't go skinny dipping. It sure doesn't in my bible. You may do what you want, but I'm sticking to my guns. I have a case and you don't. Now this conversation is over. Good day."

"Okay, I'll see you court. We'll see who's the smart one," Mike said as he stomped away.

Later that afternoon, a refreshing thunderstorm cleared the air of the heat and humidity. Rachel corralled Jamal and said, "Let's go up to the Fishers and see how Janelle is feeling."

"Oh, Mom, do I have to?"

"Yes, she's a nice girl and you should be as concerned about her health now as you were yesterday."

"But yesterday was different. She needed me."

"Well, she needs you now, too. She'll look different today."

"I'll say."

"I'm real proud of you, Jamal. You helped Janelle and she said you were a real gentleman."
"Mom, what else could I do? She was naked. He was beating her. I couldn't let it go on."

"That's right. Now may I ask, what do you think of a nude woman? Did you like it?"

"Mom, seeing a woman naked on TV or the movies is one thing. They're just actresses. Seeing Janelle was not sexy or cute. My only thought was saving her."

"That's just what I wanted to hear, son. You're a very good son and I'm am very proud of you. Now put on some shoes and let's go visit this innocent siren you just saved."

Rachel smiled at her son. She knew she had brought him up right.

They walked up to the Fishers' home. Donna met them at the back door.

"Is Janelle around? How is she feeling?" asked Rachel.

"She's still a little tender in spots, but I think most of her welts will heal without scars. She's out back swinging. Jamal, why don't you go talk to her while your mom and I have some iced tea. Tell her to come in, too."

Jamal walked to the back yard. He found Janelle swinging in her tree swing. She flowed back and forth, her eyes closed as if she were dreaming. Her long brown hair swung in the breeze with her arc. Her gown, which was three sizes too big for her, was pinched between her legs, but on one side a split opened to her thigh. As she moved forward, the split moved up and revealed she was well-tanned all the way to her waist. He couldn't tell if she was wearing anything under the gown or not.

Jamal quietly walked toward her. He stepped behind her path. He loved to see her enjoy the motion. He enjoyed her wearing a gown. It looked so womanly. When was at the apex of her backswing, he whispered, "Janelle."

She opened her eyes and stared right into his. He was only eight inches away.

"Jamal," she screamed as she returned on her downward arc. She was about halfway up again when she bailed out and fell to her knees, then sideways on the grass. The split side of her gown flew over her head, exposing a very bare leg all the way to her waist. Jamal ran to her and helped her recover. He pulled her skirt down, but he noticed the ugly red marks on the back of her legs from the beating.

"Are you okay?"
Janelle this time was blushing, but she stammered, "Y-y-yes. Where did you come from?"

"Mom said I should check on you. She's in the house with your mom."

"I guess I did it again. Gee, Jamal, I'm glad you don't have a camera. You see, I'm not wearing any underwear. If fact, all I have on is my Mom's nightgown. It is the only thing I can wear that doesn't rub my skin. It is way too big on me. See the way it dips in front. I'm almost exposed. And when I bend over like this I show everything." Janelle stopped at mid way through her bending over and stood straight, then she continued, "Jamal, why am I showing you all this? I must be nuts. I might as well take it off when you're around."

Jamal just smiled. He had just viewed his cute neighbor from her chin to her tummy and there was nothing hiding her figure.

"Well, get your mind out of the gutter, I'm not taking it off. Let's sit on the porch. I'll get us some iced tea."

Janelle walked ahead of Jamal. He noticed she limped slightly.

"Are you sure you feel okay? You're limping."

"I'm just sore."

"Does your back feel any better?"

"Some. Mom puts a salve on it three times a day. It is supposed to help with the healing and maybe take away any scars."

"I can see the one across your shoulders. It really looks red and painful."

"You should see my whole back. It's a mess. I have a bad cut under my arm. I guess I got that when I fell trying to run. I must have got some dirt in it because even after the nurse cleaned it, it still feels sore. You want to see my back?"

"No, it's all right. I can imagine what it looks like."

"No, no, it doesn't bother me. Here, you stand on the top step and pull my gown out and look down."

She turned around and hiked up the front to make the back loose.

"Now take your one hand and pull my gown away."
Jamal followed her instructions. He pulled the fabric away and looked down her back. He could see everything on her backside. It wasn't pretty. There were red welts and scabs covering her back and hips.

"Wow! How do you sleep at night?"

"On my stomach with nothing on. I may cover with a sheet, but that's all. Now let's have that iced tea."

Jamal sat in the glider while Janelle poured some drink. She found a pillow and sat by Jamal. She looked him with the eyes of a cat about to catch a mouse.

"Jamal, I don't know, but I feel so safe around you. I feel just like a sister and not a friend. I guess that is why I'm sitting here with you in a too big nightgown which just about leaves me naked. So if I am your long-lost sister, I'm going to act like one."

Jamal turned his head and studied her face. Yes, she was right. The gown she wore was very revealing. A little bit lower in front and her nipples would pop out. The slit from the bottom almost went to her waist. She was beautiful and not inhibited.

"What do you mean by that statement?"

"Now, don't take this wrong, but you have only one hand. You're my one-armed bandit. You may be able to play football in high school, but only when coach thinks the game is won or lost; otherwise, you will ride the bench. Furthermore, no college will be interested in a one-handed player. You could try basketball, but how are you going to grab rebounds and guard the opposition? But, Jamal, you do have tremendously long, strong legs. They could carry you to college. Many colleges have cross-country teams and track teams. They don't receive a lot of publicity, but they do give out scholarships. I don't plan on receiving any athletic scholarships. My black girlfriends on our team kid me and say I'm good, but I don't have the right color skin. They laugh when I call it discrimination."

Jamal didn't reply to her comments. He just studied her.

Finally, he asked, "Do you have some paper? I'd like to sketch you."

Shocked at his question, Janelle answered, "Sure. Do you need a pencil, too?"

"It would make it easier," he answered with a grin.

She hurried inside and found some paper and pencils in her father's office. She handed them to Jamal and asked, "I'm not doing this naked, am I? 'Cause if I am, you're out of luck."

Jamal laughed. "Of course not, I don't need to see you that way. I already have. Just stand still for a few minutes, so I can get an outline."

Janelle obliged.

"Now face me and pull your gown tight around your waist."

"Like this."

"Yeah, like that. Now hold it just a minute. Got it."

"Let me see."

"No, not until I have it finished. Now twirl."

Janelle spun around, letting her gown flow out. Her tanned legs showed beneath the hemline. She loved the coolness of the garment. Her mother and Rachel appeared at the door.

"How are you two doing? We hear you laughing out here."

"Jamal is doing a sketch of me. I guess I'm posing."

Rachel looked at the sketch and smiled. "It is a very good likeness. Now I'm afraid we'll have to go. He can come back and finish it."

"But I want to see the drawing."

"Not until I'm finished. Maybe in a couple of days."

A couple days came and went. Janelle forgot about the sketches. It was time to begin the fall sports program and band practice. Football and cross-country started at the same time. Janelle was excited as her mother dropped her off at high school. This was the first time she would be officially introduced to the upperclassmen. Her biggest surprise was in the car which pulled in right behind. It was Jamal and his mom.

He called, "Hi! Janelle, bet you didn't think you'd see me here."

Janelle was shocked because Jamal had always talked about football. This morning was easy. It was to get to know you, hand out practice and meet schedules, and check your physical papers from your family doctor. "This morning we'll just do five times around the track. Tomorrow we get serious and run five miles on the route I showed you."

The boys must have had the same instructions, for they began to circle the track a few minutes after the girls. Janelle waited for Jamal on the sideline. She caught his eye and waved him over.

"How come you decided on cross-country instead of football?"

"I thought about what you said, little sister. Maybe you are right. I am handicapped, but my legs still work fine. I like to run, so I'm going to give it a try. Maybe we can share rides this semester."

"Okay."

"Oh, I've been meaning to tell you. I finished the sketches. Why don't you drop down and I'll show them to you?"

"Great! I'd like that. Maybe tomorrow?"

The next day was the typical late summer Georgia scorcher. Janelle put on a sleeveless blouse, short shorts, and flip-flops and hopped into the UTV. She drove to Jamal's. He was mowing the lawn as she pulled in the drive. He waved, then hollered at her when she stopped, "Go on in. I'll be done in a minute."

Janelle went inside and called, "Rachel, are you here?"

No answer.

She heard Jamal shut down the mower. Soon the door opened. Jamal appeared in the doorway. His body was wet and shiny from sweat. His shorts were soaked through. He paused a moment, then said, "Why don't you fix us some lemonade while I take a shower? You'll find a pitcher in the refrigerator. Mom's not home."

He dashed upstairs and returned with clean clothes to dash downstairs and shower. Janelle poured lemonade and pulled up a chair. The kitchen was clean but dated. The appliances were avocado, the counter top was some sort of tile, and the table was wood. White cottage curtains covered the windows. It was pleasant and clean. She waited and listened for Jamal. She heard the shower running, then shut off. There was some grumbling, followed by, "I'll be there. Pour my lemonade."

Jamal appeared wearing thigh-length shorts and no shirt. He was barefoot. His curly black hair glistened. He sat across from her.
"I heard you grumbling. What was that about?"

"Oh, nothing."

They talked and kidded each other. Jamal located a fan to move the air a bit more. As he bent over to turn it on, his shorts slid down and showed a plumber's butt. Janelle surmised the grumbling was that he forgot to get clean underwear. She said nothing.

"I came to see those drawings. May I see them?" she asked.

"Sure, they're upstairs in my room. Let's go."

Janelle followed him up. His room was small with slanted ceilings. There was a single twin-sized bed, a desk, chair, and one window.

As he scrounged around in his desk, Janelle chose his bed. She pulled her legs up under her and looked around. All around the room were sketches of black women wearing evening gowns, dresses, and swimsuits. There were sketches of women wearing native African costumes.

"How do you like my room?" he asked.

Janelle was flabbergasted. "These are fabulous. I didn't know you were an artist. Where did you find all these girls to pose for you?"

"I didn't. You are my only real live model. The rest I got from looking at photos online and in magazines. I would like to do some more of you someday. You have a common body."

"What do you mean, common body?"

"Most models are rail thin. They don't look, in my opinion, like a real woman or girl. Here are the sketches I made of you."

He handed her a folder with several papers in it. She thumbed through and stopped at a sketch of some men in chains.

"Why this one, Jamal?"

"Oh, I was just playing around one day. I'd read stories of my relatives being shackled. My mom even has some pictures of her grandpa as a slave."

She turned to the next one. She gasped.

"This is of me when I was tied and beaten."
Janelle studied the drawing. It was of her. She had her hands tied and out in front with a rope leading in from the edge of paper. Her head was down and her hair covered her face, but her naked back showed many stripes and cuts. It was obvious she had nothing on. Jamal even had some blood dripping from the wound under her arm.

"You're not supposed to see that one. I drew right after the episode at the pond. I didn't want to forget you and how beautiful you look, even when you were all beaten and hurt."

"But Jamal, I looked terrible. My hair was a mess and I certainly was under a lot of stress."

"I know, but I drew what I saw. The inner beauty you have."

At that moment, Janelle's mood changed. Her bright smile left her face. Big tears formed in her eyes. She looked at Jamal. Her lower lip trembled.

"What's wrong, Janelle?" he asked.

"Oh, Jamal, I was so scared. I was sure Bert was going to drown me. What else could he do? He had to get rid of me. There was nothing I could do. You saved my life, Jamal. I'll be forever indebted to you."

Jamal had seen his mother and grandmother cry when his dad died, but never someone else, especially Janelle, a person he knew as someone always happy and bubbly. He didn't know what to say. He just held out his arm to give her a hug. She rose from the bed and encompassed his body. By now she was sobbing. Jamal tried to do his best to console her by patting her back. She just pushed against him harder. He could feel her soft breasts on his chest. It was something he had never experienced before. As he petted her, she reacted with an "Ouch."

"Did I pinch you?" he asked.

"No, but you rubbed my sore under my arm."

"Oh, sorry. I thought you were healed."

"No, I've got three bad scars left. One across my shoulders, one under my armpit, and one on my butt."

He tried to make her feel better by saying, "Well, they'll go away and soon it will be just a bad memory."

"But you don't realize where these are. You're a man. It doesn't affect you. You men don't wear bikinis or halter tops. You aren't concerned about bras. You just don't understand."

Jamal was taken back by her comments. He thought he was saying the right words.

"I suppose I don't understand you anymore than you understanding me not having a left hand. You have it easier. You will only have some small scars."

Janelle glared at him and backed away. She clenched her teeth.

"I'll just show you a girl's problem, Jamal Simpson."

She abruptly turned around and unzipped her shorts and pushed them to the floor. She gave them a quick kick up to the bed, then she unbuttoned her blouse and let it fall from her shoulders. She faced him and did not try to hide her body, even though she was naked to her waist. Jamal just stared at her.

"As you can see, I'm not wearing a bra. It cuts my wound too much. See the top scar. The doctor told me eventually it will be just a small white line, but the next one is right where my bra would be. I have to ask my mom to put some gauze on it every time I go out in public. It is especially tough when I run. The last one you can't see right now, so I'll show you."

She pulled the back of her underwear down about four inches. There was another ugly scar.

"This one is right at my bikini line. I will have to wear full-coverage bottoms for a long time, maybe forever. This is what I'm worried about."

"But Janelle, you're alive. These will heal in time. I'm so glad you are here. You're my best friend. I want you to stay my best friend. I love you like a sister."

With that statement, Janelle melted. She turned around and hugged Jamal again. She pressed against his bare chest, skin to skin. Jamal was surprised and pleased. His neighbor girlfriend was still his neighbor girlfriend. This feeling of her breasts against him gave him feelings he had never experienced before. He felt a lump forming inside his shorts. He pushed Janelle away and ran for the little half bath between the bedrooms. Janelle stumbled backward and fell on the bed. She was stunned for a moment, then realized what had happened. As she started to dress, she heard water running in the sink. She paused. She was just buttoning her top when Jamal emerged from the bathroom with a sheepish look on his face. He was wearing only a towel.

"Sorry," he apologized.
Janelle could barely keep from giggling. She put her hand to her mouth, but she couldn't stifle her emotions.

"Jamal Simpson," she blurted out, "you just got a hard-on and I'm the reason for it. I'm impressed. I thought you seeing me half-naked wouldn't bother you, but I guess I was wrong."

Jamal was so embarrassed, he didn't say a word.

"Did you have a mess in your shorts? My sister told me about boys having 'cream in the jeans' when she and her boyfriend get into heavy petting."

"Yes, you call it that, I suppose. I've never had it happen before," Jamal said as he turned away from her and started to open a dresser drawer.

"I'd like to see you without the towel," teased Janelle.

"In a minute." Jamal looked back at Janelle sitting there with her top half open. "When I get my shorts on.'

"No, right now," she said with a giggle in her voice. She reached over and pulled the towel away. Jamal reacted by cupping his hand over his privates as he straightened. Janelle had an excellent view of his muscular backside.

"Turn around," she kidded. "You've seen me. Why can't I see you? Come on, chicken."

"No."

"Maybe I can help. What if we are both naked? Then would you turn around?"

"Maybe, but you're a girl."

Janelle didn't waste any time. She slipped her top off and pushed the underwear down. She approached her almost bare friend and rubbed against his backside. She wrapped her arms around his middle.

She cooed, "Jamal, this isn't going to hurt. Please let me see you."

Jamal slowly turned and faced Janelle. He scanned her young body and let his hand drop. They stood quietly for several minutes. Not touching, just studying.

Jamal spoke first. "You are beautiful, Janelle."

"You're pretty handsome yourself, my naked friend."
Janelle moved toward him and pressed against his body. She stood on her tiptoes and kissed him.

Janelle smiled and said, "This is our secret. I will never say anything about this to anyone but you. Do you agree?"

"Yes, most definitely. You are the most amazing girl I will ever meet, Janelle, and I hope we stay friends forever."

"Me, too."

Janelle hurried home with memories which would stay with her forever.

Janelle's wound under her arm would not heal, so her doctor sent her to a wound clinic in Atlanta. She would have to go for several treatments. The worst part was she was to avoid high-energy sports and sweating. Thus her cross-country days were over for the year. Jamal, on the other hand, became a top runner. He won the district meet and placed fourth at state. His legs were going to carry him forward.

Bert's father dropped the charges against Jamal on the advice of his attorney. The lawyer said he better use his money to defend his son. The trial was set for January 20.

Both parties agreed on a judge deciding the verdict instead of a jury. This was a juvenile case. It was thought a judge could render a fair judgement. The courtroom at the county courthouse was small. There were a few spectators, but otherwise just family members. In the court area at one table sat Mike Coffman, Bert, and his attorney, Jim Deering. Directly behind them sat Millie, Missy, Becky and Ellie. At the other table sat Paul Fisher, Janelle, and their attorney, Carol Habersol. Rachel, Jamal, and Donna, Janelle's mother, sat behind them. At the front of the room was the court recorder's table, the judge's chair, and the sergeant of arms. Everyone waited for the judge to enter.

Finally, the sergeant of arms rose and called, "All rise. Presenting the honorable Judge Corletta F. Harper."

The judge entered. She was a small black woman with salt and pepper hair. She took her seat and said, "Please be seated."

Mike Coffman rolled his eyes and mumbled, "Just our luck, a black bitch for a judge."

His lawyer turned and stared at him. Millie reached across the railing and touched his arm. Mike jerked it away and glared at her.
The judge noticed the commotion and asked, "Is there something you would like to say, counselor?"

The attorney answered quickly, "No, Your Honor, we are good. Sorry for the noise."

The trial started with the rules and what was to be expected. Decorum was emphasized. Janelle was the first witness. After a few preliminary questions, Carol asked her to tell the judge about the beating. She showed photos of Janelle's back, her wrists, and feet. Janelle explained in detail her beating.

Carol then asked if that person was in the room.

"Yes," answered Janelle.

"Would you point him out to the judge?"

Janelle pointed at Bert.

Carol ceased her questions. It was time for the defense.

His only question was, "Miss Fisher, were you swimming naked in the pond when Bert arrived?"

"Yes."

"No further questions."

Jamal was the next witness called by Janelle's lawyer. After preliminary questions, she asked him, "How come you decided to be at the pond that day?"

Jamal replied, "Bert's sister, Missy, was across the road from our mailbox. She was crying. I asked if I could be of any help. All she said was Bert was going to get Janelle Fisher and if she told on him, he would kill her kitten. The kitten she held was already dead. I figured I better follow him as fast as I could. I got there a little late. He had already beaten Janelle. Her hands were tied and he was leading her towards the pool. I heard him threaten her by saying he would drown her in the pool beneath the falls. Janelle pleaded with him to change his mind."

"So you intervened, even though Mr. Coffman is much stronger than you."

"Yes, ma'am, but he is slower. I just had to out-quick him."

"How long have you known Bert?"
"Let's see, about eight years. They moved in when I was eight."

"Did you play with him as a child?"

"A few times, then I quit."

"Why did you quit?"

"One day I was going over to his place and he met me at the gate to his yard. He told me I shouldn't come over anymore because his dad didn't want him playing with a one-armed nigger. I had never been called that before. I hurried home and told my mom. She just said some people are that way and not to be upset."

"What about Janelle Fisher?"

"Janelle! She is like a sister to me. She scolds me and advises me. She never notices we have different skin color. She's a doll."

"Thank you, Jamal. I have no further questions."

Judge Harper spoke. "Mr. Deering, do you have any questions for the witness?"

"No, Your Honor, I have none."

Attorney Haberson rose and said, "I rest my case."

Mr. Deering called Coach Rhodes to the stand. After the preliminary questions, he asked the Coach about Bert's character and workmanship. The coach was very positive about Bert.

Next Mr. Deering called Bert to the stand. He asked about his relationship with Jamal and Janelle. Bert said it was okay. After showing Bert as a good guy, he turned and said, "Miss Haberson, your witness."

Carol started, "Mr. Coffman, do you like Janelle Fisher?"

"Yes."

"Have you taken photos of her without her knowledge?"

Bert paused.

"Must I remind you, Mr. Coffman, you are under oath to tell the truth. I repeat, did you take photos of Miss Fisher without her knowledge?"
"Yes."

"Did you put these photos on your Facebook page?"

"Yes."

"Are these some of those photos?"

Carol Haberson turned on her laptop and flashed photos of Janelle running, sunbathing in her yard, walking down a corridor in school, and several others.

"Did you stalk her?"

"Objection."

"Sustained. Please, Miss Haberson, rephrase your question," the judge requested.

"Mr. Coffman, do you think Miss Fisher is pretty and nice?"

"Yes."

"Why?"

"I think she is pretty, but lately she has refused to be friends."

"How do you know that?"

"She won't let me sit by her on the school bus. At lunch, if I come close to her table, she moves. One time she called me a bully. She doesn't like me."

"Is this the reason you watched her so closely?"

"I guess so."

Miss Haberson proceeded to the evidence table and picked up a plastic bag containing a cellphone. She asked, "Mr. Coffman, is this your cellphone?"

She handed Bert the bag. He handled it and realized on the back was his name stuck on with printer tape.

"Yes."

"I'm going to show Judge Harper and the rest of the court some photos which were found on your cellphone."
Carol flashed one photo of Janelle sitting by the Miller's Falls pool with her feet in the water. The next one showed her swimming nude in the water. Janelle hid her face. The photos were very embarrassing. The third was Bert taking a selfie and Janelle was standing waist deep in the water holding her arms across her chest. The final shot was of her standing naked with her wrists tied with a rope. They were stretched above her head because the rope was thrown over a low branch. It just showed her backside.

"Do you remember taking these photos?"

"Yes."

"All right. Mr. Coffman, do you know what it feels like to be whipped with a willow switch?"

Bert started to perspire. He looked directly at his father. He turned his eyes to his mother. He spoke softly, "Yes, I do."

"I couldn't hear you. Would repeat what you just said."

He clinched his teeth and set his jaw, then answered in loud voice.

"Yes, I do. I know what it feels like to be whipped."

"Would you like to tell the court how you know this?"

"Objection. This is not relevant to my client case."

"Judge Harper, I am asking because Mr. Coffman may have reason for his actions which the court does not realize. It may reveal the underlying cause."

"It is a little unusual, but in this case, I'll allowed it. Proceed."

"Mr. Coffman, is there someone in this room who has issued this type of corporal punishment."

"Yes."

"Would you tell the court who and point that person out?"

"He is my father and he is sitting right over there," said Bert, pointing his finger.

At his statement, Mike Coffman stood up and tipped over his chair backwards. He screamed, "I did not. I never beat my kids. He's lying. The damn kid is lying."

Attorney Deering tried to settle Mike down. Judge Harper slammed her gavel on her desk and hollered, "Order in my court. Mr. Deering, contain your client or I will have him thrown out of the room."

Mike Coffman continued to rant, "But he's lying. I never would hurt my family."

Missy sat directly behind her father in the gallery. She could take no more. She rose and cried, "Yes, he does, Mrs. Judge. He has beaten me and Becky and little Ellie. One night he came home drunk and Mommy didn't have his supper ready. He took her outside and tied her to a tree and whipped her terrible. It began to rain and he left her hanging there. Her top was in shreds. She was bleeding badly. Me and Bert carried her in. I treated her back. When Daddy got home, he was drunk and furious. He beat both me and Bert."

Mike turned and slapped Missy so hard she fell down between the seats and the railing. Millie dove for her daughter to protect her. She received a backhand from her husband. She looked over the railing and her mouth was bleeding. The courtroom was in chaos.

Judge Harper ordered, "Sergeant, arrest this man now."

Old Henry Dole was the deputy in charge. He hurried to the defendants' table and tried to subdue a much stronger and younger Mike Coffman. Mike grabbed the older man's holster and gun. He pushed Henry backwards into the jury box. Henry fell backwards. Mike now had a weapon. He pointed it at the Judge.

"You black bitch, no way you should be judging white people. You are just a prejudiced nigger."

He pointed his weapon at the judge and fired. Fortunately, it was high. The judge dove under her bench. The recorder scrambled to the floor, but before she did she hit the panic button, calling for help. Mike fired again, this time at the deputy, who was trying to stand. The bullet hit the railing beside the fallen man. Bert was still in the witness stand. He knelt and peeked over the railing. His father threatened him with the gun. Bert disappeared.

"You'll never get me, you S.O.B.," screamed Mike as he backed out of the courtroom. He fired one more shot at the judge. This time the bullet pierced the paneling in front of her desk. As he continued his retreat, Mike didn't realize the doors of the court were locked. He pushed on the door. Nothing happened. He kicked at the door. The deputies outside the courtroom surprised him by opening the door and grabbing Mike as he passed through. They pushed him to the floor. As Mike hit the floor, the gun discharged again, hitting Rachel, who crouched between the chairs, in the thigh. The projectile glanced off her bone and buried itself in the bottom of the chair next to her. Mike was immediately arrested and dragged from the room, cussing and swearing.

Back in the courtroom, Missy crawled out from under her mother. Her nose and mouth were bleeding. Judge Harper crawled out from her big chair. Deputy Dole got to his feet and hurried over to the judge.

She stopped him and said, "I'm okay. See how the young woman is doing."

"Which one?" asked Henry.

"What do you mean?" replied the judge.

"I think one of them is wounded. I heard her scream."

By now, Donna had recovered and knelt by Rachel. Rachel was in a great deal of pain, but not bleeding badly. She was holding her leg.

Donna called to Judge Harper, "This lady needs medical attention."

"It's on the way," was her answer.

The courtroom was soon full of officers and EMTs. Judge Harper looked over at Bert crouching low in the witness stand.

"You okay, son?" she asked Bert. He nodded.
Judge Harper rose and left her chair.

Deputy Henry rose and said, "All rise."

Judge turned to him and scolded, "Hush, Henry. Skip all those formalities. We have people to attend to."

Within minutes the courtroom was cleared. Judge Harper signaled the two attorneys.

"Can we meet sometime next week to discuss this case in my chambers?"

The pair nodded affirmative.

The next two weeks were a whirlwind of activity. The attorneys settled with a plea bargain. Bert would agree to attend a facility in South Georgia for troubled teens and if he completed the program successfully, the charges against him would be dropped. Rachel stayed in the hospital overnight. She returned home on crutches and would require therapy. Missy was treated and released to her mother's care. Mike Coffman was confined to jail. His trial would not occur for six months.

The day after Rachel returned home, Millie crossed the forbidden road and brought Rachel a casserole and two pieces of pie. She felt so guilty about her husband's actions. Rachel tried to assure her there were no hard feelings. The next day, Millie brought more food. Rachel commented that it was delicious. Millie replied she used many of her mother's recipes. She was so happy to use them for someone other than her family, because Mike would not allow her to go anywhere without him. This was the first time in her married life she felt free.

Rachel returned to her restaurant called the Cozy Corner Café. Although not able to work, she could still manage and greet customers. The morning Rachel returned, her head kitchen cook was involved in a motorcycle accident and would be unable to work for several weeks. Rachel panicked before realizing the perfect replacement was her neighbor, Millie. She called Millie and explained the situation. Millie was only too happy to help. She could start immediately. Rachel asked, "Like today?"

"Yes," was the answer. "Just give me a few minutes to change clothes."

Millie was fantastic. Her food was delicious. She started to bake pies using her own recipes. The Cozy Corner Café couldn't keep enough pies on the shelves. Rachel went next door to the bakery and asked if Millie could use their ovens. To her surprise, the baker said, "I'm seventy years old and would like to retire. Why don't I just sell it to you?"

Rachel agreed and Millie had her own bakery, baking pies, sweet rolls, cakes, and many different kinds of bread. News of her baking spread fast in the small town of Bremerville.

Millie filed for a divorce from Mike in June. He accepted with the statement he was doing it under duress. He would make amends later. His trial was delayed until October. He was found guilty of attempted murder and sentenced to twenty years in prison with no chance for parole for ten years.

Bert Coffman was sent to a troubled teens facility named Re–enact Acres. At first he was not happy, but soon he adjusted to the routine. He found he enjoyed working with engines, all kinds of engines, small one cylinder to the V-8s. When he returned home the next December, he not only was a changed teen, but he also realized he had to help his mother survive. He got a job after school and on weekends washing trucks at the local timber trucking company. Soon he was greasing and changing oil. His boss liked his work ethic and let him off in the fall to play football for Bremerville High. At the end of his senior year, the company offered to send him to tech school, but Bert saw more opportunities in the U.S. Army. Upon graduation he enlisted and after basics he was assigned to the motor pool.

Jamal continued his running for BHS. He won the districts twice and in his junior and senior years he won state. It was after the state cross-country finals that his coach approached him and asked if would be interested in running for a major university.

"Sure!" was Jamal's answer.

A few minutes later, a man in a red and gold jacket followed his coach.

"I'm Curtis Cashman, head coach for the cross-country team at Iowa State University. I would like to have you as part of the Cyclone team."

Jamal's first question was, "Where's is Iowa State located?"

The coach chuckled and replied, "It is in Ames, Iowa. About the middle of the state. We are a member of the Big 12 Conference. I think you'll find we compete with the best, and we tend to be in the top four contenders for the title year in and year out. I would like to fly you and your parents to State for a visit. I believe you will find it a very nice campus and a wonderful educational opportunity. By the way, what are you interested in your future career?"

"I would like to get into clothing and fabric design. I know it is a little unusual, but my teachers say I have a talent."

"Excellent. We have one of the top colleges in Human Services. It used to be Home Economics. If you decide to visit, bring along some of your work. I'll arrange for someone to review it."

Jamal took the coach to see his mother. He was so excited he could barely stand still. He never thought he'd ever be asked to run for any college. During the Thanksgiving break, he and his mom visited ISU. They were impressed with the training facilities and coaching staff. Jamal was escorted around campus by one of the team members, while his mother met with some of the coaches' wives. Dr. Heather Hanson stopped by to review Jamal's drawings. She was more than impressed.

The first words out of her mouth were, "If Coach Cashman doesn't give you a scholarship, we will. These drawings are spectacular. You have an amazing talent."
Before Jamal left the campus, he signed a letter of intent to become a Cyclone runner the next fall.

Janelle did not do as well in the running department, but her grades carried her to many scholarships at Georgia State. She entered the education field, majoring in high school and junior high natural sciences. During Christmas break of her sophomore year, she was surprised by a visit from Jamal. She was just finishing her shower when he arrived.

Her mother called up the stairs, "Jamal's here. You'd better come down."

Janelle hurried to finish. She put on some underwear, her robe, and fuzzy slippers. It was only Jamal, she thought, why get dressed. With her hair in a towel, she entered the kitchen. She hugged Jamal, then noticed there was another young man standing by the door. He was about six feet tall with a reddish beard. He had an infectious smile. She backed away and exclaimed, "Jamal, who's this?"

Jamal answered, "This is my roommate, Kent Lynch. He's in Forestry. I thought maybe your dad might take him on a tour of the plant."

Janelle went over to Kent and said, "Hi, I'm Janelle. Pardon my appearance, but I didn't know Jamal was bringing a guest. Please excuse me and I'll go upstairs and come back more presentable."

Kent had a smile from ear to ear. He replied, "You're okay. I have three sisters and they run around dressed like you a lot."

Janelle vanished to her room. When she returned, her dad was home and engaged in a conversation with Kent. Jamal saw her enter and gave her the thumbs up.

Kent turned around and spoke. "My, Janelle, you look wonderful. I hope we can see more of each other."

Janelle smiled back and said, "Thank you, Kent. I was hoping the same."

It was the start of a long-distance romance. Janelle saw Kent one more time at spring break, then in the summer he interned at the plant and stayed at Jamal's. Janelle and Kent's seeing each other was not a problem. They became great friends. When Janelle graduated, she accepted a teaching position in Tipton, the town next door to Bremerville. She taught two sections of middle school natural sciences and three sections of biology in the high school. Much to her liking, Kent found a job with the same lumber company her father worked for. He was hired as a forester in the southern region of the company's holdings.
Jamal surprised her one more time during the summer after she graduated. He visited her home just like before, but this time Janelle was prepared. When she met Jamal, she also met Lorilea. Lorilea was a tall, slim, beautiful woman. Her features were fine and she had the longest fingers Janelle had ever seen. Her black hair was tied in a bun at the back of her head. She had a smooth complexion. When Janelle shook her hand, she noticed a ring on her finger. It wasn't very big, but it had to be significant.

"What a beautiful ring?" she exclaimed. "Does it mean anything?"

Jamal butted in, "It is our pre-engagement ring. I couldn't afford a real engagement ring, so this one will have to do until then."

"You're engaged?"

"Well, not exactly," chimed in Lorilea, "but we're working on it."

Janelle turned to Jamal and asked, "How did you catch her?"

"Well…" stuttered Jamal.

Lorilea cut him off by saying, "You should ask, how did I catch him? Your friend Jamal is in great demand. He graduated at the top of his class and was recruited by several companies. During his last year, he sold several designs for children's clothing to different firms, so we decided to try and launch our own company. I will be his model and business manager. I graduated with a business degree in marketing. I have been modeling women's fashion for three years. My jobs will finance our start."

"Wow!" exclaimed Janelle. "I never expected that from my little one-armed bandit."

Jamal added, "Because of you, Janelle, we are going to name the company One-Armed Bandit's Clothing LLC. The label will read 'Bandit's Duds.'"

Janelle was so excited for the couple. She almost forgot to tell them. "Kent got a job at the lumber company. He going to work with my father. Someday, I hope, we can get married."

The trio chatted for a while. Jamal asked if Janelle had heard anything about Bert.

"Funny you should ask," she replied, "I just talked to his mom yesterday. Bert is being deployed to Iraq next month. He will be there for a year. He is now a sergeant and in charge of the motor pool. She is a little concerned, but he assured her he is not in harm's way."

"I'm glad he found his niche. He wasn't really a bad guy, just misguided by his dad."

The summer flew by, and school was about to start. Janelle was on her way home from her new teacher's orientation. She decided to stop at the

Cozy Corner for a piece of Millie's pie. The first room was full, so she entered what used to be part of the bakery. Rachel had connected the two shops for convenience and extra floor space. Janelle chose a table in the corner next to the window. Missy came over and to take her order.

"You work here?" she asked Missy.

"Only after school and weekends. Mom needs the help. She has two women baking for her in the back. Ellie and Becky even help some. She is really busy, but it is the first time she has had money to do something. Dad always controlled her life. He was mean. I'm so glad he is in prison. Sometimes I wake up at night crying because of the beatings we received when he was around. Mom still has scars on her back from his lashing," Missy said as tears formed in her eyes.

"That's over now, right?" asked Janelle.

"Oh yes, he's gone for at least ten years."

Missy returned to the back of the counter and cut Janelle's pie and poured her a cup of coffee. Janelle was daydreaming by looking out the window. A man entered the café from the bakery side. He looked around as if checking the customers, then he turned and fiddled with the entry door. He sat down in the first booth. Janelle thought he looked familiar, but couldn't place him. He was medium height and his head was shaved. He had a crooked smile on his face which she had seen before. *Who is he?* she thought.

Missy came to wait on the new customer. She stopped about three feet away. Her face showed shock. The man gazed at her.

He said, "Well, well, if it isn't my little Missy. My, you have grown into a lady. I haven't seen you for five years."

"D-d-d-dad! Why are you here? How did you get out?"

"It's a long story, but here I am. Is your mother around? I'd like to speak with her."
Missy hurried to the kitchen. The man got up and went to the passageway between the two restaurants. He closed the door and locked it. As he returned, he spotted Janelle.

"Well, if it isn't my brazen little hussy of a neighbor. Have you been swimming lately? Looks like you would fill out a bikini pretty good."

Janelle recognized the man and said, "Mr. Coffman, I thought you were in jail. How come you're here?"

"I'm here to pick up what belongs to me, then I'm out of here."

Janelle was about to carry on the conversation when Millie arrived.

"Mike, why are you here?" she asked.

"I've come to take you and the girls with me to Mexico. I've got friends down there and I want to show them my wife and kids."

"Mike, I'm not your wife anymore, remember? We're divorced."

"Oh no, we aren't. Remember 'till death do us part' in our vows. You're still mine."

"Sorry, I'm not your slave anymore. In fact, I even took my maiden name back. I'm now Millie Purcell. Now please leave, or I'll have to call the cops."

Janelle was listening to the conversation and realized this could get ugly. She began to dial 911 on her cell phone.

Mike turned to her and hollered, "Put that thing away!"

Janelle continued. Mike pulled a police baton from under his jacket and swung at Janelle's phone. He hit it directly and smashed her fingers on her left hand. The phone went flying across the room. Janelle grasped her hand and began to rise and go after her phone.

"Sit down, hussy," he ordered as he pushed his baton into her stomach and shoved her back across the chairs. Janelle crumbled into the corner. She hit her head on the corner of another chair and was stunned. She lay there, her feet in the air, her skirt almost to her waist. Mike screamed, "I'll get to you later."

"Leave her alone," screamed Millie. "Now get out of my shop."

"Not until I get what is mine. Now come here."
Mike grabbed Millie by the apron she was wearing and pulled her close. He attempted to kiss her. She turned away. He grabbed again, this time catching the top of her uniform. He ripped it open. She slapped him. He responded by hitting her in the ribs with the baton. Millie coughed and looked over at her helper, Coretta.

"Coretta, call the cops," she ordered.

Coretta reached for her cell, but before she could dial Mike threw a sugar container and hit her directly in the face. She dropped the phone and fell to her knees behind the counter. Mike returned to Millie and hit her again. She tried to protect her head with her arms, but his blows drove right through them. Finally, one blow caught her head, and she started to stagger. Mike shoved her across the room and into the pie safe. It came crashing down on top of her. Seeing Millie was no longer a threat, he turned his attention to Janelle. He grabbed her leg and began to pull her from under the table. He was furious and out of control.

"Now I'll show you how a real man takes care of whores," he snarled.

Janelle hung on to the table leg. Mike grabbed her skirt and pulled. The skirt had an elastic waistband and Mike ripped it from Janelle's body. He threw the skirt away and it landed on the counter. He reached over and slapped her face. Janelle let go of the table leg to protect herself. Mike was on top of her like a cougar on a deer. He sat on her legs as he ripped open her blouse and pushed her bra up to her neck. He was just about to attack her underwear when he heard, "That's enough, Daddy. Let her go or I'll shoot."

Mike looked up and there was Missy with a pistol in her hands. She held the gun straight out in front of her. Mike backed away from Janelle and he smiled.

"You wouldn't shoot your old dad, now would you?"

"Only if I have to. Now get out of here."

"Okay, okay, I'm going, but not before I see what you're made of. You've grown to be quite a little lady. Maybe you should show your old dad what you've got."

Mike lunged at Missy. She fired the gun. Blam!

He had a very surprised look on his face. He clutched his chest.

Blam! Blam! Missy fired twice more. Mike fell backward into the hallway.

Rachel, in the other part of her café, finally had located the passage key and unlocked the door. She hurried past Mike and hobbled to Missy. The police were pounding on the door. Coretta stumbled to the door and unlocked it. Missy stood stunned.

"Put the gun down, child," said Rachel. "It's over."

Missy slowly lowered her weapon and laid it on the counter. She started to sob. Rachel held her and let her cry it out. Coretta rushed to Millie, who was coming to. She was a mess of blood and bruises. Officer Sam House arrived and lifted the pie safe from Millie.

He called to his partner, "Call for an ambulance and more help."

He and Coretta tried to make Millie comfortable. He looked at Janelle lying between the tables. She was trying to gather her clothes around her.

"Susie, when you get through come over and help his young lady under the table."

Officer Susie grabbed a table cloth and covered the nearly naked Janelle.

"Are you okay?" she asked.

Janelle answered, "Sort of. I think I have a broken finger and maybe a couple of loose teeth. Do you know where my skirt is?"

"It over here behind the counter," said someone. "I'll bring it."

Rachel had Missy sit down. The EMT checked Millie. She was alive. Chief Sam Booth arrived. He knelt by the body of Mike. He felt his pulse and shook his head.

"He's dead. I just got a bulletin from the state police about him and two others escaping from a work crew. They figured he'd head this way."

It took a few minutes to quiet things down. Chief Sam walked over to Missy and said, "I'm afraid I'm going to have to arrest you for murdering your father."

Coretta burst out and scolded, "Sam, if you arrest her, I'll shoot you myself. This young lady is a hero. She just saved her mother, Janelle, and me from further injury or maybe death. I'll take her home with me and get her little sisters, too. You just take care of that deadbeat on the floor. When Missy feels like it, we'll come down to the station and fill out whatever you need filled out."
Sam knew Coretta meant business and didn't say a word.

Millie spent two days in the hospital. She had many bruises, two broken ribs, a lacerated eyelid, and cuts from the glass from the pie safe. Janelle had two broken fingers and several bruises.

The worst thing that happened was someone snapped a photo of her in her underwear as she waited for her skirt. It got posted momentarily on

Facebook. It was quickly pulled from the media site.

Mike Coffman was buried in Kentucky where his family was originally located. Millie drove the girls to the burial but didn't get out of the car.

The shop closed for three days to clean up the mess. It made national news and soon the café was doing more business than it could handle. Rachel set up tables and chairs outside on the sidewalk. She hired three more young women from high school. Rachel was the spokesperson for the shop. She handled the press and fed them all some of Millie's pie.

School started for Janelle the next week. She had to deal with many questions from the students about her taped fingers and bruised face. One student asked about her photos on Facebook, but seemed more concerned about her health than what she wasn't wearing.

Millie returned to a limited work week for a month. The blows from the baton had blurred her vision. She was home on her day off when a military vehicle pulled up in front of her home. Two men in military dress uniforms knocked on the front door. Millie opened the door and screamed. She knew why they were there.

One of the men spoke quietly. "Mrs. Coffman, we regret to inform you your son, Sergeant Bert Coffman, was killed in an attack on his column this morning in Iraq. We don't know the details, but we were told he died trying to save others. We are sorry for your loss, but he died fighting for his country."

A week later, Sergeant Bert Coffman returned home. He was buried in the Bremerville Cemetery. The report was he was in a column traveling to a city in Iraq which was under siege. He volunteered to go and repair several combat vehicles in order to have them return to base. On their way, the column was attacked. Bert pulled several soldiers to safety and loaded them in the back of a truck. He repaired the motor under fire and attempted to drive away. A sniper shot him just as he reached the safety of a rescue column. The ten men he saved all survived.

A year later, Millie, Missy, Ellie, and Becky were summoned to the White House. The President of the United States posthumously awarded the Medal of Honor to Sgt. Bert Coffman for his bravery above and beyond the call of duty.

On the first Friday of October on the Bremerville High football field, a plaque was unveiled at the entrance of the stadium. Above the scoreboard was the new name of the field, Bert Coffman Field. Janelle and Kent, Jamal and Lorilea, and many others attended the ceremony. Bert would be remembered as a hero and not a bully.

Life continued in the little town. Janelle and Kent married and had four children. Jamal and Lorilea traveled to New York, Los Angeles, Chicago, and finally settled in Atlanta. They became very successful. Rachel and Millie expanded the pie business and delivered pies to Macon, Savanna, and Atlanta. They employed ten women to help.

Life goes on, and many of the events which seemed important at the time faded. It was only at the Friday night football games where they remembered all the names of those involved.

Miller's Falls was now a distant memory. Bert went from villain to hero. Janelle never forgot her best friend Jamal, who had stayed a best friend despite his great success. Missy emerged as a strong woman and leader. She graduated from law school and returned to run for the Georgia Senate. She sponsored legislation to prevent spousal abuse.

There were many, but who was the real hero? Was it Jamal? Janelle? Missy? Or Bert?

About the Author

Bob and his wife, Jane, live on the family farm which was established 1868 by his great grandfather. The farm has grown since its beginning, from the original 80 acres to 640 acres. Bob was raised on the farm. He worked and played there all his life. The pastures and corn fields are featured in his stories. Bob and Jane raised three sons and taught them the rewards of diligent work. After farming for 48 years they retired in 2008.

He started writing some short stories. His 1st novel, The Nightgown, was short story which grew into a novel. Since then he has written four more novels, two romances and two mystery. This last book is a collection of the stories Bob wrote in his mind driving a combine or planting corn. He wanted to place them an anthology of stories for others to enjoy. They range from true stories to fantasy tales.

This is Bob Bancks' sixth book published. Other titles include:
The Nightgown
The Fourth Generation
Call Sara
Iowa Exposed
There Are Bears.

Made in the USA
San Bernardino, CA
10 November 2017